TRUSTEE FACTS FILE

Fourth Edition

Robert P. Doyle and Robert N. Knight, editors
Illinois Library Association

©2012 Illinois Library Association

e-book creation by Books & Projects, Minnetonka, Minnesota

Library of Congress Cataloging-in-Publication Data
Trustee Facts File/Robert P. Doyle and Robert N. Knight. eds—4th ed.
   p. cm.
Includes bibliographical references.
ISBN: 978-1-890249-02-1
1. Public library trustees - Illinois   I. Doyle, Robert P., 1951   II. Knight, Robert N., 1952
Z681.7.UST78 2012

Contents

Preface

The fourth edition of the *Trustee Facts File* is meant to provide a broad overview of the duties, responsibilities, and tasks of the public library trustee.

The following resources will be of great help to the interested and educated trustee:

- *Illinois Library Laws and Rules*, published by the Illinois Library Association
- annual calendar of actions to be taken at board meetings, including financial calendar
- monthly report from your director
- monthly financial reports from your treasurer and director
- copy of your annual budget
- policy handbook, which should include your bylaws
- *ILA Reporter* and the *ILA E-Newsletter,* free to all ILA members
- your system's newsletter
- *E-News*, the Illinois Secretary of State and State Librarian newsletter

Additionally, the ILA, the state library, and other organizations periodically offer workshops and seminars to library staff and trustees. These are important sources of continuing education for trustees.

Being a trustee is an important role in providing an essential service to our communities. Congratulations on accepting this job, and good luck in carrying it out.

Chapter 1

TRUSTEE DUTIES AND RESPONSIBILITIES

The Big Picture

If legions of jobseekers were vying for trustee positions on library boards, a want ad for the job might read as above.

Of course, service on a library board is pro bono public service, so you will not have arrived here by dazzling a job interviewer. As a library user and supporter, you may have campaigned for an elected trustee position, or perhaps you hesitantly accepted appointment. Either way, you have a most important job to do.

A public library might be defined as a repository of information available to all in the community. This public resource addresses and meets a wide variety of needs. For some members of the community, the library is the chief or only source for recreational reading. For others, it is a valuable professional resource. Young children discover the wide world of ideas in the library. People of all ages use computers and the Internet at libraries to prepare themselves to function in the modern digital world. Disabled people find resources in public libraries that may not be available elsewhere. You, as a trustee, represent all of these people.

A public library, even of relatively small size, is a complex operation that requires informed and skillful administration and management. You, along with the other trustees on the library board, oversee performance of these roles by library staff.

The Board of Trustees

Library trustees do their work collectively on the library board. Though the board has broad powers—it is answerable only to the governing body that has oversight over the library or, if elected, to the voters—those powers are exercised collectively. No individual trustee can speak or act for the board, or for the library, unless specifically empowered to do so by board action or adopted bylaws.

The board's crucial partner in administering the library is the library director. This professional has been hired by the board and serves at the board's pleasure. The board depends heavily on the professional judgment and experience of the director. For example, the board of trustees can draft an annual budget for the library, but specific input about what moneys are needed for which purposes comes mainly from the director. As a trained professional, he or she is employed to assess needs such as acquisitions, staff coverage, and public services.

The remainder of this chapter details duties of the board of trustees, both those assisted and unassisted by the library director; responsibilities of individual trustees; and basic rules of ethics for trustees.

Duties

Broadly speaking, the board of trustees establishes library policies, and the library director implements those policies in the day-to-day operations of the library. However, these roles are interdependent and require careful distinction of responsibility and authority.

The degree to which the board relies on the librarian's professional knowledge and experience will, of course, vary with the situation. In every case, however, cooperation is the key to a smoothly run, successful library. A library in which all the players work cooperatively toward the common goal will inevitably deliver greater benefits to the community than one in which trustees and librarian work competitively, at odds with each other. The following lists detail duties carried out collectively by boards of trustees in public libraries.

Duties of the Board Assisted by Input from the Director . . .

- Write and maintain an official mission statement for the library.
- Develop long-range plans to address anticipated community needs.
- Establish and support library policies. Examples of such policies include
  - levels of service (for example, open hours).
  - registration and circulation policies and other rules directly affecting patron use.
  - types of service (in addition to circulation and informational services, will the library provide special programs for children? the disabled? the visually impaired? or literacy training?).
  - confidentiality and privacy policies.
  - patron access to the Internet.
  - collection development policy.
- Authorize salary and benefits plans for library staff.
- Assess maintenance of library grounds and buildings, and authorize purchase of lands or construction of new buildings when necessary and appropriate.
- Develop an annual budget.
- Review monthly financial reports to ensure accountability to budget goals.
- Provide financial information and an independent audit as required by Illinois law.
- Advocate for funding necessary to meet community library needs.
- Engage in other fundraising activities as necessary and appropriate.
- Promote the library in the community.

Duties of the Board, Exclusively . . .

- Hire a qualified library director.
- valuate director's performance periodically, at least annually.
- Establish policies for the functioning of the board. Such policies include
  - by-laws governing meetings, quorums, selection of officers and the length of their terms as officers; and other matters relating to handling the business of the board.
  - finance policies (for example, how funds will be dispersed or invested, or who will be authorized to write checks).
  - trustee's code of ethics.

For more information about division of duties between the board of trustees and the library director, go online to the Illinois State Library Administrative Ready Reference, http://www.webjunction.org/partners/Illinois/il-topics/readyref.html: select **Policy Model; Board of Trustees**; select **Division of Responsibility**. . . .

You, Personally

For the library machine to hum smoothly, every participant—trustee and staff—must shoulder a fair and proper load. To carry out the trustee duties which you have accepted, you will need to make a substantial commitment of time and effort.

Your Duties as a Trustee . . .

- Attend board meetings.
- Preview agenda, minutes, and documents before each board meeting.
- Participate in discussion and decision making at board meetings.
- Stand by decisions made by the board.
- Serve on committees as assigned by chair.
- Commit time outside of board meetings for the work of the board, as necessary and appropriate.
- Participate in activities sanctioned by the board, such as fundraising or public relations in the community.
- Represent the library at community events—be visible and accessible to those you represent.
- Become informed about library issues through participation in the regional library system, ILA, and ALA.
- Become informed about state laws that govern public libraries in Illinois.
- Become an advocate for the library community.

As with any position of responsibility and accountability, library trusteeship calls for adherence to high standards of ethical behavior.

Your Ethical Responsibilities . . .

- If you have a conflict of interest in a matter taken up by the board, you must remove yourself from consideration and voting on that matter. For example, your financial stake in a firm with which the board does or intends to do business would constitute a conflict of interest. (For more information about conflicts of interest, see Chapter 4, "Legal Responsibilities and Liability.")
- Respect the opinions and contributions of other trustees; refrain from dogmatic or bullying behavior at board meetings. Work toward acceptable compromise on contentious issues.
- Do not voice opposition to board decisions in public; limit criticism to debates within board meetings.
- Respect confidential information: do not reveal content of closed session board discussions.
- Refer patron/public requests for information to the library director.
- Refer staff grievances or problems to the library director, who has full responsibility for managing staff; refrain from becoming involved in controversy or conflict among staff.
- Refer complaints from the public to the library director.
- Do not initiate or participate in ad hoc board meetings called without advance notice and knowledge of all participants. Conform to the Open Meetings Act in posting required meeting notices for the public and the press.
- Assume full responsibility as a board member. Attend board meetings regularly and perform all assigned committee work in a timely manner. If you are unable to fulfill your duties, consider resigning so that someone else can better serve.

• Support open access to information and resist moves toward censorship.

Finally, consider the benefits you will derive from serving as a library trustee. You will make new acquaintances and friendships with people who are passionate about, and dedicated to, values of public service. Some of these people will become personal friends; others will remain good professional associates. Whether you are a worker in a trade, a professional, a homemaker, an independent businessperson, or are engaged in some other life activity, the people network you establish during your tenure of trusteeship will likely prove to be of great benefit to you.

Then, of course, there is the obvious: you will be making an important contribution to the people in your community and to your community's future. A public library is one of the most universal and accessible institutions in our society. Your contribution as a public library trustee will help bring opportunity to all the people, irrespective of all the differences that sometimes divide communities in other spheres. Don't underrate the satisfaction you will derive from this endeavor.

Resources

Gale, Robert L. *Leadership Roles in Nonprofit Governance.* Washington, D.C.: Board Source, 2003.

Grace, Kay Sprinkel. *The Ultimate Board Member's Book.* Medfield, Mass.: Emerson & Church Pub., 2008.

Ingram, Richard T. *Ten Basic Responsibilities of Nonprofit Boards,* second ed. Washington, D.C: Board Source, 2009.

O'Connell, Brian. *The Board Member's Book: Making a Difference in Voluntary Organizations,* third ed. New York: Foundation Center, 2003.

Chapter 2

ORIENTATION FOR NEW TRUSTEES

This chapter has two parts. The first part, which follows immediately, is for new trustees. The second part is for anyone responsible for new member orientation, including mentoring library board member(s) and/or the library director.

So, You Are a New Library Trustee

In the following sections, you will read about types of administrative units in Illinois public libraries. Then you will read a brief history of public libraries in the United States. Your colleagues on the board or the library director will conduct your orientation to the library, its services, and resources, and will provide you with various materials you need to begin your duties as a library trustee.

Illinois Public Libraries—Administrative Types

Many public libraries in Illinois are legally established by cities, villages, and townships, according to the Illinois Local Library Act, 75 ILCS 5. In these cases, the library's service boundaries are coterminous with that of the municipality or township. District libraries, which are established within independently defined boundaries, are the alternative to municipal libraries.

In towns, villages, and townships, citizens establish public libraries by referendum. Most towns and villages elect their library trustees; in villages with the commission form of government, the village council appoints library trustees.

In cities, the city government establishes a public library, and the mayor appoints trustees. Illinois law allows mayors to appoint one city council member to the library board, among a total of nine library trustees.

District libraries are public libraries established under the Illinois Public Library District Act, 75 ILCS 16. A district may include area from more than one local governmental unit and outlying unincorporated areas. District libraries have independent corporate authority and taxing power for support of public library services. Like other library administrative units, district libraries are run by a board of trustees.

The following table gives more detailed information about boards of library trustees among the various types of local libraries.

Trustee Service by Type of Administrative Unit

Type: City
Trustees Appointed/Elected: 9, appointed by mayor
Term of Service: 3 years

Type: Village/town/township
Trustees Appointed/Elected: 7, elected
Term of Service: 4 or 6 years

Type: Village with commission government
Trustees Appointed/Elected: 6, appointed by village council
Term of Service: 6 years

Type: District
Trustees Appointed/Elected: 7, elected
Term of Service: 4 or 6 years

A Brief History of Public Libraries

In early colonial America, academic pursuits were largely allied with the education of clergy. The first significant library in the colonies was Harvard College Library, founded in 1636 with a gift of about 300 mostly theological books.

An important expansion of the concept and role of a civic library occurred in 1731 when Benjamin Franklin and other Philadelphians established a subscription library in Pennsylvania's chief city. In a subscription library, patrons pay a subscription, or fee, to use the pooled reading material of all the subscribers. Further distinguishing the "Library Company of Philadelphia" was the collection's emphasis on travel, philosophy, and biography, rather than religious topics.

Truly public libraries—open to all free of charge—were the creation of the United States in the new democratic age of the nineteenth century. Inspired by the founding of the new nation, the adoption of First Amendment free speech principles in the Bill of Rights, and extension of democratic expression and personal freedoms in the early years of the republic, the movement for universal public education gained momentum by the mid-1800's, creating demand for free public libraries as well. In 1854, Boston opened the first big-city public library funded by local taxes. In 1872, the Illinois General Assembly passed legislation authorizing tax-supported public libraries. Soon thereafter, public libraries were organized in the Illinois municipalities of Chicago, East St. Louis, Elgin, Moline, Oregon, Rockford, Rock Island, and Warsaw.

In step with these developments, librarian Melvil Dewey in 1876 helped establish the American Library Association (ALA), helped found the *Library Journal*, and published the Dewey Decimal classification system. In 1887, Dewey established the nation's first library school at New York's Columbia University. In 1896, the Illinois Library Association (ILA) was established.

As the twentieth century dawned, public libraries in the United States began to benefit handsomely from the philanthropy of steel tycoon Andrew Carnegie, whose charitable foundations eventually built about 1,700 libraries. Carnegie libraries were built in communities that agreed to provide land for building a library and to contribute some funding on an ongoing basis. By the 1920s, public libraries were widespread throughout the United States, with publicly funded institutions in most towns of any size.

An important trend beginning in the mid-twentieth century has been involvement by the federal government in public libraries. Since the 1950s, Congress has allocated funding for rural library extensions, library construction, expansion of school libraries, provision of services for people with disabilities, and Internet connectivity, among other services.

In the last half-century, technology-driven developments have transformed public libraries in many ways. The new technologies have led to nearly universal computerization of card catalogs. Electronic and digital materials such as DVDs have enhanced library collections. In all but the smallest library branches, Internet access for patrons has become standard.

New services have posed new challenges. Internet connectivity offers potential access by minors to websites with inappropriate content, for example. Congress has responded by tying libraries' eligibility for certain federal funds to installation of filtering software. (See Chapter 6, "Intellectual Freedom," for more information on Congressional mandates codified in the Children's Internet Protection Act, or CIPA.)

Today, some 9,000 administrative units in the United States offer public library services in over 16,000 libraries, including branches. Our state of Illinois has 637 public libraries—796 if you count total branches and buildings. These public libraries endeavor to serve their changing communities in a variety of ways as they strive to maintain free and open access to information.

Congratulations.

You have completed your first step of orientation as a library trustee. The remainder of this chapter is primarily for your board member colleagues or the library director who are responsible for further orientation activities.

Planning Orientation for a New Trustee

The preceding part of this chapter provides background material that will help new library trustees put into context the duties they are about to assume. Have inductees read the material as part of their overall orientation activities.

Your library board should have a well-defined, written orientation plan in place. If it does not, suggest that the board establish a committee to draw up such a plan.

The following sections provide guidelines for orientation of new library trustees. The first section outlines orientation activities. The second lists materials that the board or library director should provide to new trustees.

Orientation Activities

The board president, or her/his designate from the board, will make the initial contact with the new trustee to schedule orientation sessions. First and foremost should be a get-acquainted tour of the library with library staff. The library director or a management level staff person should conduct the tour, providing a "big-picture" overview of collections, services, and general policies. The director should introduce available staff members, explaining their duties.

The board president or her/his designate will then schedule an appointment with the inductee for an introduction to the business of the board, including bylaws; ethics; meeting times and formats; recent decisions and accomplishments; future plans and goals; and budgets.

Orientation for the incoming trustee might well extend into the next scheduled board meeting. For example, the board president might conduct business at a slower pace, encourage experienced board members to describe accomplishments of the past year, and allow time in the meeting for the new member to ask questions (no meetings after adjournment, even if informal, if a quorum is present).

Orientation Activities Summarized . . .

- Activities conducted by the board president:
  - initial contact with inductee to schedule orientation
  - introduction of the bylaws and other business of the board
  - review of duties of the board and of the director
  - presentation of budget and other financial information
  - planning the agenda of the next scheduled board meeting so as to accommodate the information needs of the new member (if feasible and appropriate)
- Activities conducted by the director:
  - tour of library facilities
  - introduction of library staff members

Orientation Materials

Eventually, new trustees will need to master the wide range of information relevant to governing the public library. Because the volume of such information is necessarily large, it is useful to focus on a smaller subset of such materials during the initial orientation. Following is a suggested list of materials for new trustees.

Orientation Materials List . . .

- Library mission statement
- List of board members and the director, including address, telephone number, and e-mail addresses
  - Indicate terms of office and identify officers.
- Calendar of board meetings and library holidays
- Organization chart of library staff
- Illinois Library Association *Trustee Facts File* (the publication you are reading)
  - Have inductee read Chapter 1 and the first part of Chapter 2 (this chapter) initially.
  - Draw attention to subsequent sections of the *Trustee Facts File*, as appropriate.
- Board of Trustees bylaws (reference the *Trustee Facts File*, Chapter 3)
- Library policy manual (reference the *Trustee Facts File*, Chapter 5)
- Budget for current and previous year (reference the *Trustee Facts File*, Chapter 10)
- Annual report, most recent available
- Monthly reports, most recent available
  - financial report: dispersal of monies
  - statistical report: volume of circulation, etc.
- Minutes from recent board meetings (reference the *Trustee Facts File*, Chapter 3)
- *Illinois Library Laws & Rules* (copyright 2012)
- *Serving Our Public: Standards for Illinois Public Libraries*, 2.0 (copyright 2009)
- Recent issues of the *ILA Reporter*, which can be obtained online from www.ila.org/store/ila-reporter
- Information about the Illinois State Library, regional library systems, and their relationships to local libraries
- Contact information, including website addresses, for the American Library Association (ALA), Illinois Library Association (ILA), and Illinois State Library (See Appendix G, "Selected Resources.")
- Local library history, if available
  - Append to the general history of U.S. public libraries in the first part of this chapter.
- Promotional materials—for example, the latest issue of the library newsletter or newspa-

per articles about the library and its services (reference the *Trustee Facts File*, Chapter 13)

Resources

Hughes, Sandra R., Berit M. Lakey, and Marla J. Bobowick. *The Board Building Cycle: Nine Steps to Finding, Recruiting, and Engaging Nonprofit Board Members*, second ed. Washington, D.C.: Board Source, 2007.

Kurtz, Daniel L. *Board Liability: Guide for Nonprofit Directors.* Mt. Kisco, N.Y.: Moyer Bell Limited, 2007.

Moore, Mary Y. *The Successful Trustee Handbook*, second ed. Chicago: American Library Association, 2010.

Reed, Sally Gardner and Jillian Kalonick. *The Complete Library Trustee Handbook.* New York: Neal-Schuman Publishers, 2010.

Sturgis, Alice. *The New Standard Code of Parliamentary Procedure*, fifth ed. New York: McGraw-Hill, 2011.

Chapter 3

BOARD ORGANIZATION

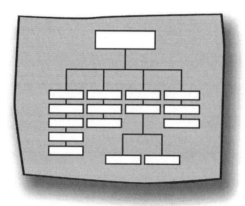

In Chapter 1, you became acquainted with duties of library boards collectively as well as duties of individual trustees. This chapter focuses on the board's collective responsibilities and the organizational means available to execute those responsibilities. Before proceeding further, you might want to review in Chapter 1 the section entitled "The Board of Trustees."

Library Board Bylaws

Every library board should establish *bylaws*, a set of rules that define the structure and function of the board and its operational procedures. The bylaws should be recorded in clear, unambiguous language. Board trustees should review bylaws annually and amend them as necessary. The bylaws of a public library board in Illinois must not conflict with federal or state laws.

The following list summarizes topics that the bylaws should address.

Contents of Bylaws . . .

- The name of the board
- The constituency served by the library and its board
- The composition of the board
- Procedure for election or appointment of board trustees
- Terms of board trustees
- Procedure for filling an unexpired trustee term
- The schedule (frequency) of board meetings
- Procedure for calling special meetings of the board
- Specification of a quorum

    A quorum is the minimum number of people who must be present in order for a deliberative body to transact business. There is no set quorum for library boards; each board establishes its own definition of a quorum in its bylaws. For example, a 7-member board may specify 4 as its quorum; so the trustees may transact business at a board meeting if 4 or more members are present.

- Summary of duties and powers of board officers
- Identification and description of standing committees
- Procedure for setting up special (ad hoc) committees

- Order of business for board meetings
- Rules of conduct for board meetings, such as *Robert's Rules of Order*
- Procedure for amending the bylaws

To view a sample set of library board bylaws, go online to the Illinois State Library Administrative Ready Reference, http://www.webjunction.org/partners/Illinois/il-topics/readyref.html: select **Policy Model; Board of Trustees;** select **Bylaws of the XYZ Public Library**.

Board Meetings and the Open Meetings Act

The Illinois Open Meetings Act (5 ILCS 120) specifies that public bodies in the state of Illinois exist "to aid in the conduct of the people's business and that the people have a right to be informed as to the conduct of their business." The law mandates that deliberations and actions of public bodies be conducted in public, and that citizens be given advance notice of and the right to attend such meetings. The law defines a "meeting" as "any gathering of a majority of a quorum of the members of a public body held for the purpose of discussing public business."

Under state statutes, a library board is a "public body." Therefore, board meetings and board committee meetings must be open to the public and conducted on days convenient to the public. It would not be proper, for example, to schedule a board meeting on a federal holiday. Effective January 1, 2012, elected or appointed members of a public body subject to the Open Meetings Act must complete the electronic training once during their term of election or appointment. The Public Access Counselor's Office's Open Meetings Act electronic training is available free of charge at: http://foia.ilattorneygeneral.net/electronic_foia_training.aspx.

To conform to the requirements of the Open Meetings Act, library boards should publicize the schedule and location of regular meetings at the beginning of each calendar or fiscal year. The media may request a schedule as well. Boards should post the agenda for each meeting in a public area of the library 48 hours in advance of the meeting time.

When conducting an open meeting, make sure that library doors are unlocked. Let members of the public in!

Closed ("Executive") Sessions

A library board in the state of Illinois may meet in a closed, or executive, session if such a meeting is approved by "a majority vote of a quorum present" during a meeting that is open to the public. The closed session should be listed on the meeting's agenda.

The board may schedule a closed session, for example, to consider any of the following matters: (1) negotiation for the acquisition of real estate, (2) the possible hiring of an individual, or (3) salaries of classes of employees. See the text of the law—5 ILCS 120/2 (c)—for more exceptions to open meetings. Information discussed in a closed session is to remain confidential until/unless the matter is revealed or acted upon in open session by the board.

To ensure the legality of all board meetings, discussions, and communications, trustees should become familiar with the requirements of the Open Meetings Act.

Officers of the Board

As stated previously, bylaws should clearly identify officer positions of the board and define the duties of each office. Most library boards require four officer positions, those of **president (chairperson), vice-president, secretary,** and **treasurer**.

President (Chairperson)

The president, working closely with the library director, prepares agendas for board meetings for distribution to participants in advance of each meeting. The president presides at board meetings, serving as discussion leader, and appoints committee members. He or she signs official documents and may under instruction from the board represent the library at public meetings and gatherings. When the board president speaks on behalf of the library, he or she must reflect the adopted positions of the board, not personal views. As a single member of the board, he or she has one vote.

Vice-President (Vice-Chairperson)

The vice-president presides at board meetings in the absence of the president and performs such other duties as are assigned.

Secretary

The secretary records the proceedings of meetings, then prepares written minutes and issues them to trustees in advance of the next meeting. After the minutes of a past meeting are approved, the secretary prepares a permanent and correct copy for the archives of the library. The preparation of the minutes may be assigned to staff, but if delegated, the process is completed with the oversight of the board secretary. The Illinois Open Meetings Act mandates that minutes of all board meetings—including closed (or executive) sessions—must be prepared and archived. The minutes of open sessions should be kept in a secure but accessible location in the library and made available to the public upon request. Twice a year boards must consider whether to open minutes of individual closed sessions or keep them closed.

Treasurer

The treasurer's role typically depends on the size of the library. In smaller communities, the treasurer may handle funds, keep books, and prepare reports on the general finances of the library. In larger libraries, the treasurer is a legal officer named to assure that the financial operations of the library are handled properly, including oversight of annual audits. The board treasurer should prepare or assist in the preparation of annual budgets and chair the finance committee. By law the treasurer is bonded or insured in an amount not less than 50 percent of the total funds received by the library in the last fiscal year for all libraries except those municipalities over 500,000 in population (75 ILCS 5/4-9 and 75 ILCS 16/30-35e).

Committees

Most library boards delegate detail work to committees to save the time of the full board. Such committees prepare recommendations for the board's decision, but do not make those decisions on their own. If lengthy or complex, committee reports should be submitted in writing in advance of a board meeting.

Standing committees generally deal with ongoing and long-range concerns of the board, such as facility maintenance, finance, personnel, public relations, and fund raising. Special or ad hoc committees are created to deal with short-term or one-time tasks.

Committees are subject to the Illinois Open Meetings Act; therefore, their meetings should be conducted in public with appropriate advance public notice, and minutes of meetings must be recorded and archived.

Agendas

When not well planned, meetings tend to digress and waste participants' time. The board president should develop a meeting agenda and distribute it in a timely fashion before each board meeting. The following is a sample agenda.

A Sample Agenda . . .

- Call to order; recording of attendance; determination of quorum
- Review of minutes from previous meeting; call for corrections or additions; motion to accept minutes
- Treasurer's report/authorization for the payment of invoices
- Library Director's report
- Board President's report
- Committee reports
- Public comment
- Unfinished business
- New business
- Closed Session (best to keep on the agenda permanently so the session is always in order if needed)
- Items for the next agenda
- Announcements
- Adjournment, with announcement of date, time, and place of next meeting

Resources

Chait, Richard P. *How to Help Your Board Govern More and Manage Less*, revised edition. Washington, D.C.: Board Source, 2003.

Dambach, Charles F. *Structures and Practices of Nonprofit Boards*, second ed. Washington, D.C.: Board Source, 2009.

Flynn, Outi. *Meet Smarter: A Guide to Better Nonprofit Board Meetings*. Washington, D.C.: Board Source, 2004.

Tesdahl, D. Benson. *The Nonprofit Board's Guide to Bylaws: Creating a Framework for Effective Governance*. Washington, D.C.: Board Source, 2005.

Chapter 4

LEGAL RESPONSIBILITIES AND LIABILITY

Legal Status of Library Trustees

As a library trustee, you have become a member of a public body—the board of trustees of a public library. In Illinois law, a public body is defined as a legislative, executive, administrative, or advisory body that expends tax revenue (5 ILCS 120).

As a public servant, you enact the role of a fiduciary—that is, a person who holds something in trust for others. A public library is a community asset that you and the other board members, in your fiduciary role, hold in trust for the public. Violations of that trust could result in legal consequences for you and other trustees. Such violations might include active errors, as for example, exceeding legal authority; or passive errors, as in failing to meet responsibilities to provide a safe, accessible library environment.

Illinois law endows library trustees with specific powers and duties. The Illinois Local Library Act (75 ILCS 5/4) and the Public Library District Act of 1991 (75 ILCS 16/30) summarize powers of library boards of trustees.

At minimum, a library board of trustees holds the following legal obligations:

A Library Board's Basic Legal Obligations . . .

- To organize the board with written bylaws and elected officers
- To meet regularly in conformance with the Illinois Open Meetings Law (See Chapter 3, "Board Organization.")
- To provide written minutes of every meeting of the board and its committees and to archive the minutes after approval by the board
- To prepare and maintain audio or video recordings of closed (executive) sessions of the board
- To provide bonding of the treasurer or other person designated by the board to receive and disperse funds
- To submit an annual report to the host municipality, i.e., village, township, or city (for local libraries only; does not apply to district libraries)
- To submit an online annual report in compliance with the requirements of the Illinois

State Library
- To conduct all library business in accordance with federal, state, and local laws

Trustees should become familiar with the following laws and be certain to meet their requirements:
- Americans with Disabilities Act (ADA)
- Fair Labor Standards Act (FLSA)
- Minimum wage
- Prevailing wage
- Family Medical Leave Act (FMLA)
- Health Insurance Portability and Accountability Act of 1996 (HIPPA)
- Drug-free workplace

Trustees and the library director should work with their regional library system, the Illinois State Library, and ILA to monitor new laws or revisions to existing acts.

Risks of Liability for Library Trustees

A library board of trustees has legal status similar to that of a corporation: it can enter into contracts and take title to property under a specific legal name, such as "The Board of Library Trustees of (name of governmental unit)." Like other corporations, the library board can sue—and it can be sued.

So long as a trustee is operating within the lawful authority of his/her position, a trustee will not be held personally liable for his/her actions. However, there is no way to prevent someone from individually initiating a suit against a trustee. For that reason, library boards typically purchase insurance against liabilities related to the public library, and Illinois law specifically authorizes library boards to purchase such insurance. Insurance companies offer policies specifically tailored to protecting public officials. Such policies may be called "directors and officers liability" insurance or "errors and omissions" insurance.

For a sample policy to insure library trustees and staff against liability, go online to the Illinois State Library Administrative Ready Reference, http://www.webjunction.org/partners/illinois/il-topics/readyref.html: select **Policy Model**; select **Financial Policies**; select **Indemnification & Insurance**.

Liability may result from injury or harm that a person receives while on library property. If a library patron falls on a slippery floor and breaks an arm, for example, that person might have legal ground to sue the library board for damages. Liability may also result from malfeasance committed by one or more library trustees, in gross violation of trustee fiduciary responsibility. The section of this chapter entitled "Ways to Minimize Risks of Liability" will help you understand how to carry out your board responsibilities properly so as to minimize legal risks.

Trustees may be held liable for actions committed by staff employees. For example, if a staff member destroys library records in violation of Illinois statutes mandating retention of such records, the board could be held legally liable. The same might be true if a staff member commits a discriminatory act against a patron. For these reasons, a library board should carefully and in good faith exercise its responsibility in hiring a library director who understands the legal implications of library administration.

Conflict of Interest: An Invitation to Liability

A situation known as *conflict of interest* arises if any library trustee or trustee relative or associate receives any gain, tangible or intangible, in the course of the trustee's service on the library board. Conflict of interest is one of the most serious forms of public malfeasance, and it may be prosecuted criminally. Liability may well extend to board members other than the perpetrator, if there is any appearance of collusion or even passive tolerance.

The following are examples of situations in which there is a conflict of interest.

Example: The library board enters into a contract with a company that will provide a service to the library; a trustee on the board is a relative of the company president.

Example: A library trustee accepts a gift from a person or entity that could have an interest in the conduct of library board business.

Example: The board hires one of its trustee members, an attorney, to provide legal counsel.

Example: The board purchases a lot for library construction from a real estate company with which a trustee is associated.

Ways To Minimize Risks of Liability

Collectively, the board of trustees can conduct its business in such a way as to minimize risks of liability. The following lists summarize steps trustees can take to minimize risks of liability as a board and as individuals.

How The Board Can Minimize Risks of Liability . . .

- Comply with all provisions of the Illinois Open Meetings Law (5 ILCS 120) to ensure that all meetings, records, and communications meet statutory requirements.
- Comply with the state Officials and Employee Ethics Act (Public Act 93-615 and 93-617), which requires the adoption of an ordinance or resolution regulating political activities and solicitation and acceptance of gifts by library officers and employees.
- Rigorously avoid any conflict of interest, even the appearance of such.
- Ensure that the library is operated in a safe manner. Maintain physical facilities properly. (See Chapter 9, "Facilities.")
- Hire a qualified library director and perform annual evaluations that include a review of staff management.
- Carefully follow any procedures established by the board for the avoidance of personal conflicts and the reporting of ethical violations.
- If aware of a legal or ethical violation, contact the appropriate executive or law enforcement agency.
- If unsure of any legal obligation, seek the advice of an attorney, and when appropriate, consider seeking an advisory opinion from the Illinois Attorney General's office.
- Establish legally defensible library policies. The following are examples of policies that could be construed as indefensible:
  - The library imposes extreme penalties; for example, a patron has library privileges revoked for a minor infraction, such as bringing food or drink into a posted off-limits area.
  - The library engages in a practice that might be viewed as discriminatory, such as enforcing policies differently for identifiable groups (homeless visitors, minority groups, etc.)
- Post library rules and regulations openly.
- Review financial records regularly. Submit financial records to annual audit, as provided for by law.
- Conduct regular audits of meeting minutes. Such audits ensure that these important records are complete, accurate, and approved by appropriate signature(s). An audit of the secretary's minutes is a requirement of the district library's annual report sent to the state library.
- File all mandatory reports promptly.
- Ensure that all library policies and regulations conform to federal, state, and local laws.

- Retain services of an attorney to advise the board from time to time on legal aspects of board business and decisions.
- In board proceedings, follow standard rules, such as *Roberts Rules of Order*.
- Establish library policies and practices to ensure that public queries or complaints will be addressed promptly.
  - For example, if an individual or group within the community protests availability of a particular material, alleging that the material is offensive in some way (for example, obscene), the board's designated representative will respond to the specific complaint. The person so designated—the library director, for example—should be able to mount an effective response based upon codified library policies, law, and public libraries' commitment to freedom of information.
- Review liability insurance coverage annually to determine whether it is adequate.

How You Can Minimize Your Risks of Liability . . .

- Carefully avoid all possibilities of conflict of interest.
- If you suspect conflict of interest on the board, make a written record of protest, such as a letter to the board president. Committing your protest to writing may protect you from liability.
- If an issue comes before the board for a vote and you do not yet have the information you need to make a decision, request a tabling of the issue or abstain from voting.
- Review minutes to affirm that they accurately represent your statements and votes. It is especially important that an accurate record of member voting be kept.
- Perform your trustee duties to the best of your ability and in good faith.
- Actively seek information about new or changing laws that will apply to the library.
- If unsure about legal issues, consult an attorney for professional advice.
- Remember that the board operates as a team and not as individuals. As individuals, board members have no authority, except for that specifically delegated by the board.

Resources

Hopkins, Bruce R. *Legal Responsibilities of Nonprofit Boards*, second ed. Washington, D.C.: Board Source, 2009.

Illinois Library Laws & Rules. Chicago: Illinois Library Association, 2012.

Minow, Mary and Thomas A. Lipinski. *The Library's Legal Answer Book*. Chicago: American Library Association, 2003.

Torrans, Lee Ann. *Law and Libraries: The Public Library*. Westport, Conn.: Libraries Unlimited, 2004.

Chapter 5

POLICYMAKING

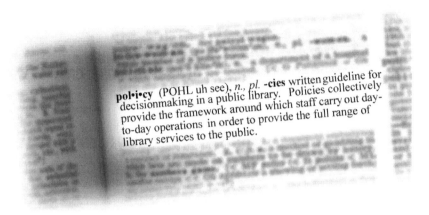

pol•i•cy (POHL uh see), *n., pl.* **-cies** written guideline for decisionmaking in a public library. Policies collectively provide the framework around which staff carry out day-to-day operations in order to provide the full range of library services to the public.

Like other public institutions, a library must endeavor to meet public expectations in a consistent, efficient way. A library with haphazard hours, a disorganized collection, and a confused staff would be of little use to the community. The most important tools with which library trustees and staff provide effective service to the community are written, codified policies. Because the public collectively owns its public library, the library's written collection of policies is made available to all.

More specifically, a comprehensive set of well-defined, well-written policies is important to a public library because it

- guides trustees and library staff in carrying out their duties.
- helps ensure high-quality service to meet community needs.
- communicates privileges and duties regarding library use to the public.
- helps ensure fair treatment of all patrons and staff.
- helps ensure conformity to local, state, and federal laws.

An excellent source for policy models is available on the Illinois State Library website: go online to the Illinois State Library Administrative Ready Reference, http://www.webjunction.org/part-ners/Illinois/il-topics/readyref.html: select **Policy Model**.

Policies Versus Procedures

A policy, as defined above, is a written principle for guiding trustees and staff in providing the full range of library service to the community. A *procedure* is a specification of the steps needed to carry out a specific task. The library board of trustees develops, approves, and codifies all policies, based on input from the library director or other staff. In most cases, effective boards delegate procedural work to the library director and staff. Policies tend to be broad statements of intent, while procedures deal with specifics—the "nuts and bolts." The following graphic summarizes the differences between policies and procedures.

Summarizing Differences Between Policy and Procedure

Policy

Definition: Written statement to guide trustees and staff in providing library service to the public
Example: The library's Green Room shall be made available for public use in one-hour blocks (renewable) on weekends.
Author: Board of Trustees

Procedure

Definition: Specification of the steps needed to carry out a particular task
Example: The library staff maintains a sign-in book for weekend use of the Green Room and tracks the usage.
Author: library director or other staff (typically)

How the Board Makes and Codifies Policies

The crafting of a specific policy is usually prompted by a specific problem or need. Often, the issue is brought to the board's attention by the library director or other staff member—the people "on the front lines" of library administration. The board discusses an appropriate policy response, writes a policy draft, and revises the draft after further discussion. The board or its appropriate committee also codifies new policies; that is, dates, numbers, and files them appropriately. The following flowchart summarizes the policymaking process.

Policymaking Flowchart

Identify problem or need
Receive staff input
Solicit community input
Discuss in board meeting
Assign to board committee
Committee drafts policy statement
Board considers policy statement
Board approves policy
Board codifies policy

Standards for Policies

Policies can be crafted—and written—well or poorly. Well-designed, well-written policies should
- be stated unambiguously.
- be capable of being applied consistently and fairly.
- be reasonable and capable of being implemented.
- comply with local, state, and federal laws.
- reflect the library's goals and objectives (its mission statement).
See the table "Good and Bad Library Policies" for examples of "good" and "bad" policies.

Codifying Policies

Because policies should be easily identifiable, each policy should acquire a unique identifier (number) upon board approval. Another important piece of information is the date of approval; identifier and date might be combined in a single code. Most likely the board will assign to a committee the task of managing policy codification.

All relevant policies should be maintained in online files and collected in an easy-to-update manual. The policy manual should have a table of contents and an index. Both of these features will need to be updated regularly.

Every trustee and every library staff member should receive a copy of the policy manual. In addition, the manual must be made available to the public.

Illinois law requires that important public records be retained by the library for a designated number of years. Policy manuals are included in this category. Contact the Illinois Local Records Commission for more information and assistance. (Illinois State Archives Building, Springfield, IL 62756; phone: (217) 782-7075)

Changing Policies

It is not at all unusual for libraries to revise policies periodically or even to discard them after a time. Types and levels of service change frequently, due to such factors as rising or falling funding levels or changing community needs.

Some changes in library service are driven by cultural or technological developments. Consider how cultural attitudes to gender and ethnicity have changed since the civil rights movements of the 1950s, 1960s, and later. Recall the changes technology has wrought in your lifetime.

For these reasons, it is vitally important that the library board review policies on a regular basis. One policy your library board will surely want to document is a statement of how frequently it will review policy. *Serving Our Public 2.0: Standards for Illinois Public Libraries* recommends reviewing policies at least every three years.

"Good" and "Bad" Library Policies

Subject of Policy: Loan period for books, Audiotapes
"Bad" Example: Patrons may borrow books and audiotapes for a period of three weeks or two weeks.
Critique: Stated ambiguously.
"Good" Example: Patrons may borrow books for three weeks. Patrons may borrow audiotapes for two weeks.

Subject of Policy: Loaned materials lost by patrons
"Bad" Example: Patrons who lose loaned materials may be asked to pay for them.
Critique: Leaves room for inconsistent application and unequal treatment.
"Good" Example: Patrons who lose loaned materials will be charged the cost of the materials.

Subject of Policy: Posting notices on a public bulletin board
"Bad" Example: The board of trustees will give or deny permission for all postings on the public bulletin board.
Critique: Implementation of the policy is too specific for the board's involvement; board properly establishes the bulletin board policy but does not implement it.
"Good" Example: The library will provide a self-posting public bulletin board; library staff will regularly review postings to remove obsolete items or items that do not conform to board policies.

Subject of Policy: Responding to patron challenges to particular materials
"Bad" Example: Someone from the library should respond promptly to a patron challenge to particular materials.

Critique: Not specific enough.

"Good" Example: In the case of a patron challenge to particular materials, the board will designate a staff member to contact the patron within 24 hours to explain the library's policy and procedures regarding challenged materials.

Subject of Policy: Overdue fines

"Bad" Example: The overdue fine for a book is 5¢ per day; the daily fine doubles every seven days and continues accruing.

Critique: Open to various interpretations; no fine maximum specified; policy may be unfair and counterproductive to the return of materials.

"Good" Example: The overdue fine for a book is 5¢ per day; the fine continues accruing until such time as it exceeds the replacement cost of the book. Patrons will not be charged a fine greater than replacement cost.

Areas Addressed by Specific Policies

The library board, in its policymaking role, must address a wide range of issues. The following list highlights general areas addressed by policies. The list is not intended to be exhaustive; policies not mentioned here may be addressed in the Administrative Ready Reference website, http://www.webjunction.org/partners/illinois/il-topics/readyref.html, cited in the opening section of this chapter.

Policy Areas . . .

- A mission statement
- Hours/days of library operation
- Lending rules, including registration for borrowing privileges
- Development and management of the collection
  - Collection development policy establishes guidelines for collection of new materials with recognition of different formats, age levels, multiple copies, and other factors. Guidelines must be issued for how to "weed out" damaged or obsolete materials from the collection. By law, the library board must review the policy for selection of library materials at least every two years (75 ILCS 5/4-7.2; 75 ILCS 16/30-60).
- Level of cooperation or interaction with other libraries or systems
  - Public libraries participate in interlibrary loan and reciprocal borrowing.
- Provision of specialized services
  - For example, libraries provide braille materials and books on tape for visually impaired persons; they may provide special ESL (English as a second language) services for patrons not proficient in English; or they may serve congregate living sites. Each type of service may require policies to guide operations.
- Provision of child-oriented services
  - Libraries may offer storytelling and other special activities for young children that require special policy considerations.
- Policies defining acceptable/unacceptable patron behavior
  - Such policies should be reviewed by legal counsel and include instructions for dealing with problem behaviors.
- Purchasing and disposing of library materials and other assets
- Use of computers and the Internet
- Public use of meeting rooms and display spaces
- Acceptance and use of gifts and memorials
  - See Chapter 11, "Fundraising."
- Public relations, including interaction with local media

- See Chapter 12, "Advocacy," and Chapter 13, "Public Relations."
- Human resources (personnel)
  - See Chapter 8, "Human Resources."
- Continuing education for trustees and staff
  - See Chapter 14, "Trustee Continuing Education."
- Mechanism for responding to patron complaints
  - See Chapter 6, "Intellectual Freedom," Chapter 12, "Advocacy," and Chapter 13, "Public Relations."
- Whether/how to use volunteer services
- Periodic review of all library policies
- Solicitation by outside groups or individuals (such as Girl Scouts selling cookies or petition gatherers)
- Posting of non-library fliers and announcements

Resources

Baughman, James C. *Policy Making for Public Library Trustees.* Englewood, Colo.: Libraries Unlimited, Inc., 1993.

Illinois Library Association. *Serving Our Public 2.0: Standards for Illinois Public Libraries.* Chicago: Illinois Library Association, 2009.

Nelson, Sandra and June Garcia. *Creating Policies for Results: From Chaos to Clarity.* Chicago: American Library Association, 2003.

Chapter 6

INTELLECTUAL FREEDOM

Amendment One

Congress shall make no law respecting an establishment

of religion, or prohibiting the free exercise thereof;

or abridging the freedom of speech, or of the press;

or the right of the people peaceably to assemble,

and to petition the government for a redress of grievances.

So proclaims the First Amendment to the United States Constitution, part of the Bill of Rights—the group of ten amendments protecting personal liberties—ratified in 1791 in the infancy of the United States of America. Since that time, federal and state courts have invoked the First Amendment countless times in a wide variety of situations and have extended freedom of speech and of the press to a broader concept of freedom of information, the right of every citizen to have unrestrained access to all kinds of information. This basic right is also known as intellectual freedom. (A brief glossary of terms relevant to intellectual freedom is appended at the end of this chapter.) At odds with these concepts of freedom of speech, the press, and access to information is the concept that one person or a group of persons may, under certain conditions, deprive access of others to various information. This idea is known as censorship.

Library Trusteeship and Censorship

Public libraries fulfill a unique role in the preservation of our constitutionally grounded democracy. They provide an environment in which all people can explore ideas and pursue knowledge without any government-imposed restrictions or restraints. The existence of such a resource attests to our collective belief that ordinary citizens, relying on their own critical judgment, can and should make their own choices and value judgments.

As a library trustee, you are committed to freedom of information by the oath of office that you took. Steadfastly upholding this freedom is sometimes challenging. You must freely tolerate ideas that may offend your sensibilities or contradict your personal beliefs. You may even be called upon to defend public access to such information. The willingness to do so is the ultimate test of your commitment as a library trustee.

The Selection Policy

Commitment to the principle of unfettered access to information imposes on library trustees and staff the responsibility of choosing materials in as open and unbiased manner as possible. The board of trustees is responsible for shaping a materials selection policy. This policy should include, at minimum, a clear statement of intellectual freedom and delegation of actual selection tasks to the library director or other staff.

In preparing a library materials selection policy, trustees might refer to the following American Library Association (ALA) statements on intellectual freedom (copies of these documents will be found in the Appendices section of the document you are now reading):

- ALA *Library Bill of Rights*
- ALA *Freedom to Read*
- *Freedom to View Statement*

Having a clear written statement of selection principles is a well-grounded first step in dealing with challenges to library materials.

Why Challenges Occur

Public libraries are repositories of our culture—the good and the bad. In our free society, forces contend and controversies arise. It is not surprising that the public library sometimes becomes a focus for a clash of philosophies and ideologies. People's motivations for imposing censorship may be well intentioned, but the fact remains that censors try to limit the freedom of others to choose what they read, see, or hear. Most censors' objections concern sex, profanity, and racism, and most involve concerns about children's exposure to material in these categories. While the intent to protect children is commendable, censorship itself contains hazards far greater that the "evil" against which the protection is leveled. U.S. Supreme Court Justice William Brennan, in *Texas v. Johnson*, said, "If there is a bedrock principle underlying the First Amendment, it is the Government may not prohibit the expression of an idea simply because society finds the idea itself offensive or disagreeable." Individuals may restrict what they themselves or their children read, but they must not call on governmental or public agencies to prevent others from reading or seeing that material.

A Policy to Handle Challenges

It is critically important for library administration to have on hand a written policy for responding to challenges. That policy should document a two-phase response to challenges: the first, by staff, most likely the library director; and the second, an appeal (if desired) to the board of trustees.

Adhering to such a policy ensures that the complaint will be heard, understood, and registered properly; that library representatives will have a satisfactory forum for responding to the challenge; and that complainants will emerge from the challenge process convinced that they have been taken seriously—even if the final decision goes against them.

A sample policy for responding to materials challenges is outlined here. Trustees and staff should receive training in the policy to ensure that all are prepared to handle a challenge if one should come.

Policy for Responding to a Challenge . . .

Phase 1: Library director or other staff responds

- When an individual complains verbally about a material to a staff member, the staff member directs the complainant to a senior staff member who has been trained to respond to a "Request for Reconsideration" of specific material in the library's collection. The patron should be invited to discuss his/her concerns in a nonpublic area and be thanked for taking time and effort to share them with library staff. At the end of the meeting, the staff member should request that the complainant submit his/her concerns in writing, and the staff member should explain why it is important for library personnel to have a written record of the complaints. Copies of the challenged material remain available to the public during the review process.
- The library director or other designated staff member responds to the complaint within the specified span of time and communicates a decision on the challenged material.

Though the response may be either verbal or written, as appropriate, the staff member should make a written record of the response to file permanently with the submitted written complaint.

Phase 2: Appeal to the board of trustees

- Members of the public must have recourse to a hearing before the board of trustees if they are not satisfied with the decision rendered by the library director or other staff member. The board or its designated committee should invite the complainant to appear at an open meeting to express his or her concern.
- Within a specified time period after the hearing in an open meeting, the board renders its decision, in writing, to the complainant. The board's decision is final.

Most critically, all library representatives—staff or trustees—must treat the complainant with utmost respect and politeness. The interaction should be regarded as an occasion for exchange of ideas and an educational opportunity.

Access to the Internet

The medium of the Internet is truly a "brave new world" of mass media. Anyone who doubts its power as a communications medium should consider that many of the biggest news stories in our time filter through the Internet before they hit many of the more traditional media.

As powerful a presence as it is, the Internet has often been characterized as an electronic "Wild West." Any individual or entity may freely post a website to broadcast any conceivable message, verbal or visual.

For public libraries, the Internet poses a special challenge. Unlike books and audio and video recordings, which are professionally published and reviewed, the Internet bypasses all professional principles of selection. The medium places the burden—or opportunity—of selection entirely on users.

Many parents and other child advocates have expressed concerns that the Internet affords access to material deemed unsuitable or harmful for children. They cite websites that are pornographic in nature or sites that promote hatred and violence. Some of these concerned individuals and associations advocate imposing varying degrees of censorship on Internet use by minors in public libraries.

The ALA, while fully sharing concerns for the welfare of children, opposes any such moves toward Internet censorship. The ALA's position is clearly expressed in the publication, *Libraries and the Internet Toolkit*. To obtain an electronic copy of this publication, go online to the ALA Office for Intellectual Freedom, http://www.ala.org/alaorg/oif, and select **Intellectual Freedom Toolkits**. The publication also contains useful guidelines for Internet use addressed to parents, children, and other public library users.

The Illinois Library Association (ILA) asserts that Internet policy is appropriately developed at the level of the local library rather than at the state or federal level.

Filtering Software

Some telecommunications companies and software manufacturers, responding to a perceived need in the marketplace, have developed filtering software programs. While search engines separate the relevant from the irrelevant, filtering software programs block websites considered "objectionable" according to the manufacturer's own, often undisclosed, criteria.

Companies use filtering software to control what their employees access on the Internet. Parents often use filtering software to limit what their children can access at home.

Filtering software has limitations, however. The software programs are not intelligent enough to evaluate every context in which information is embedded. For example, a filtering program may block the source websites for these titles, based on identification of the letter clusters s-e-x and n-u-d-i:

- Congress Subpoenas <u>Ex</u>-Secretary
- Photos of <u>Nudi</u>branch Specimens, Also Known as Sea Slugs

On the other hand, purveyors of pornography or other objectionable material on the web quickly adapt and defend against filtering techniques—such that even with filtering software, some of the objectionable material gets through. Filtering software may over time become more discriminating and effective, but it is unlikely ever to be foolproof.

Children's Internet Protection Act (CIPA)

The debate about children's access to the Internet entered the political arena by the late 1990s. In 2000, Congress passed, and President Bill Clinton signed, the Children's Internet Protection Act (CIPA).

CIPA ties public libraries' federal grants for telecommunications and Internet funding to implementation of filtering software on all their Internet-enabled computers, with the intent of protecting minors from objectionable Internet-based material. The so-called e-rate program, funded by a federal tax on phone companies (which is passed on to customers of those companies), provides substantial grants to public libraries to enable them to provide Internet service and other technology-based services to patrons. Many public libraries, especially those in rural or disadvantaged areas, depend primarily on this e-rate funding to provide such services.

A lawsuit contested CIPA's constitutionality in the federal courts, and the U.S. Supreme Court ultimately took up the issue. The high court ruled in June 2003 that CIPA is constitutional, but only if adult patrons in public libraries can have filtering software disabled promptly upon their making such a request. This narrow ruling left open the door for further challenges to CIPA.

What Does It All Mean for Us?

As of the publication date of this document in 2012, CIPA is the law of the land. To ensure eligibility for e-rate funding, public libraries must therefore implement filtering software on their Internet-enabled computers. Some library boards have determined that the amount of e-rate money for which they qualify is not sufficient to warrant filtered access to the Internet on all library work stations.

In general, the law requires that the public library craft and write a general policy on use of the Internet. A model of such a policy is available at the Illinois State Library's Administrative Ready Reference. Go online to http://www.webjunction.org/partners/Illinois/il-topics/ready-ref.html: select **Policy Model**. Then select **Patron Service Policies**; select **Public Access to Electronic Information Networks**.

Patrons' Right to Privacy

Along with intellectual freedom, states and localities have long upheld library patrons' right to privacy. Specifically, individuals who access information in public libraries are held to have the right to keep private all records concerning such access.

Law enforcement officials may legally gain access to library records by executing a court-issued subpoena, or by obtaining a search warrant from a judge. In Illinois, a law enforcement officer may request registration records without a court order when it is impractical to get an order and there is an emergency where the officer has probable cause to believe that there is imminent danger of physical harm. With implementation of the USA Patriot Act, passed by Congress in the wake of the September 11, 2001, terrorist attacks on the United States, the likelihood of library staff being presented with a search warrant has increased. Provisions of the act lower the threshold of probable cause in the issuance of a search warrant in cases where national security may be involved. Hypothetically, law enforcement officials might wish to access library records of an individual believed to have sought information about making explosives, for example.

Presentation of a search warrant to library staff demands a prompt, orderly response. Legally, authorities have the right to execute a search warrant without delay. However, library and legal experts advise library staff to request a brief delay and immediately seek legal counsel from the library's attorney. At the very least, the attorney should be able to validate the warrant's legality—that it is properly filled out and signed by a judge or magistrate. If the warrant is not properly prepared and signed, it may well not have legal force.

Ideally, the library administration (trustees and library director) will have the opportunity to develop a policy for responding to requests for information from law enforcement authorities before such time as a search warrant may be presented. ALA and other library advocates strongly advise public library administrators to develop such policies and train staff to implement them. An example of such a policy is available online through LLRX.com, a free web journal that provides information for administrative professionals including library professionals.

Resources

The American Library Association maintains a broad program for the promotion and defense of intellectual freedom. The ALA Intellectual Freedom Committee recommends policy to the ALA Council and sponsors educational programs.

The ALA Office for Intellectual Freedom (OIF) implements policy concerning the concept of intellectual freedom as embodied in the *Library Bill of Rights*. The OIF provides advice and consultation to individuals and libraries in the throes of potential or actual censorship controversies. The office provides reviews and information about the author of the challenged materials, applicable ALA policies, advice about the implementation of reconsideration policies, and other counsel specific to the situation at hand.

If needed, the OIF will provide a written position statement defending the principles of intellectual freedom in materials selection. As requested, the OIF provides the names of persons available to offer testimony or support before library boards. The options chosen are always the prerogative of the individual requesting assistance. The office maintains an active website (www.ala.org/oif) with many practical materials and suggestions to help cope with challenges.

The Freedom to Read Foundation (www.ftrf.org) was incorporated as a separate organization in 1969 by ALA to act as its legal defense arm for intellectual freedom in libraries. The foundation's work has been divided into two primary activities: 1) the allocation and disbursement of grants to individuals and groups primarily for the purpose of aiding them in litigation; and 2) direct participation in litigation dealing with freedom of speech and of the press.

The Illinois Library Association has an Intellectual Freedom Committee, which also provides support to those facing potential or actual censorship controversies. The committee is also charged with working with other organizations to build a state coalition in defense of intellectual and academic freedom. The current chair and committee members are listed on the ILA website (www.ila.org).
For current topics, see:
   http://www.ila.org/committees/intellectual-freedom-committee
   http://www.ila.org/advocacy/banned-books

Specific Titles

Doyle, Robert P. *Banned Books*. Chicago: American Library Association, 2010.

_____. "Confidentiality: A Case Study in Progress," *ILA Reporter*, February 2005, pp. 18-23.

_____. "Libraries as Sanctuaries for Criminals?," *ILA Reporter*, December 2006, pp. 12-17.

Nye, Valerie and Kathy Barco. *True Stories of Censorship Battles*. Chicago: American Library Association, 2012.

Office for Intellectual Freedom. *Intellectual Freedom Manual*, eighth ed. Chicago: American Library Association, 2010.

Pinnell-Stephens, June. *Protecting Intellectual Freedom in Your Public Library*. Chicago: American Library Association, 2012.

Intellectual Freedom Terms

Intellectual freedom is the right of every individual to both seek and receive information from all points of view without restriction. It provides for free access to all expressions of ideas through which any and all sides of a question, cause, or movement may be explored. Intellectual freedom encompasses the freedom to hold, receive, and disseminate ideas.

At the 1986 American Library Association (ALA) Annual Conference, the ALA Intellectual Freedom Committee adopted the following operative definitions of some terms frequently used to describe the various levels of incidents that may or may not lead to censorship.

Censorship: A change in the access status of material, made by a governing authority or its representatives. Such changes include: exclusion, restriction, removal, or age/grade level changes.

Expression of Concern: An inquiry that has judgmental overtones.

Oral Complaint: An oral challenge to the presence and/or appropriateness of the material in question.

Public Attack: A publicly disseminated statement challenging the value of the material, presented to the media and/or others outside the institutional organization in order to gain public support for further action.

Written Complaint: A formal, written complaint filed with the institution (library, school, etc.) challenging the presence and/or appropriateness of specific material.

The following definitions are from: Peck, Robert S. *Libraries, the First Amendment, and Cyberspace: What You Need to Know*. Chicago: American Library Association, 1999.

Child Pornography: Special category of sexual material that the U.S. Supreme Court has said can be prohibited in the interest of preventing commerce in the abusive use of children as subjects of pornography.

Fighting Words: Those words "which by their very utterance inflict injury or tend to incite an immediate breach of the peace." Such words must be uttered as a direct personal insult in a face-to-face confrontation and are calculated or highly likely to result in an immediate violent physical reaction.

Hate Speech: This category of "speech" receives considerable constitutional protection because the government cannot prescribe which thoughts we can think or which political philosophies we can advocate. The U.S. Supreme Court has said that the "fighting words doctrine" is not a tool to cleanse public debate or regulate words that give offense.

Libel: A written libel or an oral slander defames an individual and has the effect of ruining that person's reputation, standing in the community, or ability to associate with others. Because of the adverse economic consequences that false accusations can have, the courts can award damages to compensate an individual injured by those false accusations. By contrast, truthful yet harmful accusations incur no similar damage and are not actionable.

Nudity: Obscenity and nudity are not synonymous. Although obscene materials, which is a very narrow category of hardcore sexual acts that have a tendency to excite lustful thoughts, can be illegal, a law that prohibited the circulation or exposure of materials that contained nudity would not be constitutional. In fact, in 1975, the U.S. Supreme Court struck down a law that banned nudity in movies shown in drive-in theaters when the screen was visible from the street.

Obscenity: To be obscene, a court or jury must determine that 1) the average person, applying contemporary community standards, would find that the work, taken as a whole, appeals to the prurient interest; 2) the work depicts or describes, in a patently offensive way, sexual conduct specifically defined by the applicable law; 3) the work, taken as a whole, lacks serious literary, artistic, political, or scientific value.

Pornography: In legal terms, obscenity and pornography are not synonyms. Pornography is a form of protected speech. The U.S. Supreme Court has recognized that erotic messages are within the First Amendment's protections. The court's obscenity decisions comprehend that sex is a subject in well-regarded literature and art and a mysterious force that commands great human attention. The court therefore decided that society's concerns about obscenity should not be a vehicle to interfere with serious artistic or scientific endeavors.

Chapter 7

PLANNING

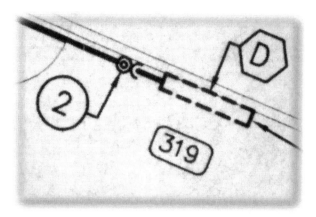

Planning is part of most our daily activities. We make a list before visiting the grocery store. We cluster errands together on days off to dispatch them as efficiently and quickly as possible. We consult the calendar to plan a social event.

Collaborative activities require greater planning efforts. As a new member of a library board, you probably are already aware of some of the planning involved in library trusteeship. At the very least, someone must schedule meetings and notify participants in a timely fashion.

All of these scenarios describe day-to-day or week-to-week planning. We might call this kind of planning "subsistence" planning. It is the planning that must be done just to get by.

There is another kind of planning. It involves looking well ahead into the future. It often requires thinking in "broad brush-strokes." This kind of planning we can call "strategic" planning.

This chapter is about strategic, or long-term, planning.

If you need to be convinced of the value and importance strategic planning in your role as a library trustee, consider:

- In the modern era, societal roles are constantly changing. We continually adapt to new expectations and opportunities. Attitudes to gender, race, disability, and other human attributes need frequent updating. In the public arena, you and your fellow trustees can't afford to fall out of step.
- We are living in the midst of a technology revolution. Whatever is "latest and greatest" today is tomorrow's has-been. In terms of technology, you and your fellow trustees simply can't afford to sit still or stand pat.
- Governments from top to bottom operate under chronic money pressures. As recipients of public appropriations, public libraries are constantly challenged to justify funding requests. If you and your fellow trustees have a clear strategic vision for the future and a well-written plan to back up that vision, you will be in a good position to advocate funding for your library.

Of course, there are many other good reasons to embrace strategic planning and do it well:

- Assures that services and activities continue to reflect the library's mission.

- Provides a context for setting priorities.
- Identifies achievements for the period and provides a "yard stick" to measure progress.
- Provides a strong foundation for decision-making if library funding or the community environment alters quickly.

The Planning Process

To do effective planning, you will need to proceed according to a rational process. The following sections summarize planning process. For more detail about planning process, consult the resources listed at the end of the chapter.

The planning process can be reduced to five basic questions.

1. What timetable will we set for ourselves?
2. Where are we now?
3. Where do we need to go, based on community needs?
4. How do we get there?
5. How will we measure our progress?

Setting the Planning Horizon

What timetable will your plan follow? What horizon will you set as the date by which stated goals will be accomplished?

A three-to-five year horizon is probably standard among most libraries. With the acceleration of technological change in our time, some library boards are opting for relatively short planning horizons. However, bear in mind the practical realities. A plan that has no hope of being achieved is sure to frustrate and disappoint. Think through this step in the planning process carefully, with ample board discussion and in full consultation with the library director.

Assessing Where We Are Now

"Know thyself," admonished the inscription at the Delphic Oracle in ancient Greece. It is still good advice.

Any serious attempt at strategic planning must start with a clear understanding of the current state of things. For you as a trustee, that probably means getting to know the library as thoroughly as you can. For the board as a whole, it may mean maintaining an up-to-date profile of library holdings, services, and programs.

An effective board should have a finger on the "pulse" of the library. Measuring that pulse will entail making at least the following evaluations, in consultation with the library director:

- List of services and programs currently offered
- Circulation and other usage statistics, including any trends that emerge over time
- Composition and age of the collection, broken down by media type and classification
- Patron service areas (for example, reference or juvenile sections)
- Staff working areas
- Technology-based offerings

And since library services are highly dependent upon available facilities, a good profile should include a physical evaluation. Input from the library director and other staff members will be critical in making such an evaluation:

- Shelving capacity
- Accessibility of all public areas to disabled persons
- Ability to meet all government codes
- Quality of lighting
- Energy efficiency
- Adequate and appropriate signage
- Security

- Parking
- Convenience of location to the community at large

Assessing Needs

A public library is, above all, answerable to the community it serves. Priority number one for library administration—the library director and the board of trustees—is to anticipate community needs and act decisively to meet them. This is a challenging, but not impossible, task.

The key is maintaining relationships and open communication with community members. The library administration should keep lines of communication active and open with "stakeholders"—some or all of the following people or groups:

- Library staff
- Current library users
- Non-user members of the community
- Business organizations, such as the chamber of commerce
- Literacy advocacy groups
- Representatives of schools and other educational institutions
- Governmental agencies
- Community planning committee
- Ethnic community organizations, especially those representing significant minorities within the community
- Family service organizations, such as a county department of social services
- Financial institutions, such as banks and credit unions
- Public health officials and representatives of hospitals and clinics
- Representatives of neighboring or regional libraries
- Representatives from media in the community
- Advocacy organizations for the disabled
- Religious groups
- Senior centers, senior service organizations, and senior housing sites
- Youth service organizations such as Boy Scouts and Girl Scouts

Obtaining Information

In addition to communicating with stakeholders, your library board will probably need to access statistical data. For example, U.S. census data provides valuable information about the makeup of communities on the basis of age, race, gender, economic status, and other measures. Another good source is the Illinois Public Library Annual Statistics, http://www.cyberdriveillinois.com/departments/library/libraries/IPLAR/home.html.

Consider carefully what other types of information is necessary to make planning decisions. You may need to conduct interviews or conduct a formal survey to elicit information more specific to your community and library. Seek only the information you need and will use, as surveys can be costly and time-consuming. Professional help is valuable, perhaps necessary.

Obtaining meaningful information in a survey can be tricky. For data to be representative of public opinion, the sample group surveyed must be randomly selected and contain enough responses. Questions must be crafted carefully to elicit useful information. The obvious question may not be the best way to encourage meaningful responses. The following is a simple example.

How To Phrase Survey Questions

Wrong way	What changes would you like to see in your public library?
Responses	Participants are likely to answer based on their own preconceptions about the library.
Right way	What do you do (occupation)? What do you enjoy doing? What are your goals for the next year?
Responses	Participants are likely to yield useful information about their own needs.

When all the data have been collected, the board will need to conduct a formal needs assessment.

A Plan That Will Get Us There

The very first part of a strategic plan is a mission statement. Your library probably already has one. Creating or reviewing the mission statement should be the starting point for planning.

A mission statement is a crystal-clear, jargon-free, concise statement of an organization's purpose, function, and values. Guidelines for writing a mission statement are widely available. You can get help from the following sources:

- *Strategic Planning for Results* by Sandra Nelson
  Source: Public Library Association, 2008
- http://www.tgci.com
  Source: The Grantsmanship Center, a company that trains people in writing grant proposals
- http://www.nonprofits.org
  Source: The Internet Nonprofit Center, sponsored by The Evergreen State Society, a civic organization based in Seattle, Washington

The library mission statement should be disseminated to everyone—trustees, staff, and community. It should be revisited and revised periodically, perhaps every three years.

Goals, Objectives, and Activities

Out of the needs assessment conducted by the board flow goals, objectives, and activities. These components form the core of a meaningful strategic plan.

Data amassed is of little practical value unless and until it can be turned into useful tools for action. A well-done needs assessment should prepare planners to turn the focus to the business of defining goals, objectives, and activities, which will in turn, enable planners to identify and embrace an appropriate action plan.

- A **goal** is a general outcome that a target population (or the entire population served) will receive through library programs and services.
- An **objective** is the way in which the library will measure progress toward a specified goal. An objective consists of a measure, a standard for comparing the measure, and a timeframe.
- **Activities** are groups of related actions that the library will carry out in order to achieve goals and objectives.

The following table provides an example to illustrate goal/objective/activity relationships.

Goal	Computer-challenged adults in the community will have access to programs to help them gain a measure of computer literacy.
Objective	During fiscal year _____, as many as 100 adults will receive basic hands-on computer training.

Activity   A two-session computer literacy class will be offered one weeknight and one Saturday in each of four "semesters."

The goals-and-objectives paradigm is common to many types of planning. The interpretation presented here is inspired by the Public Library Association's *The New Planning for Results,* by Sandra Nelson. See the Resources section at the end of this chapter for bibliographical information about this work.

Specialized Planning

Some library activities require special planning efforts, perhaps assignment to a committee of the board. Two areas of library activity that might be candidates for special attention are technology planning and disaster planning. Both of these special plans have been required by the Illinois State Library.

Components of Technology Planning . . .

- Telephone service/voice mail/faxes/e-mail
- Internet connection service and email
- Equipment: photocopiers, fax machines, microfilm readers, printers
- Computers for staff use
- Computers for patron use
- Local area network to link computers within the library
- Circulation control software; online catalogs; automated acquisitions and cataloging
- Participation in regional computer networks and databases, if applicable
- System administrator to keep all computer systems going
- Library websites
- TTY service for the hearing impaired

Components for Disaster Planning . . .

- Staff knowledge about how properly to handle medical emergencies
- Strategies in case of fire, tornado, or terrorism emergencies
- Strategy for salvaging library resources in an emergency in which the facilities are under threat
- Resource lists of services and products to aid in recovery from emergencies
- Communication plans:
  - for staff instructions
  - for informing the community

Resources

Board Source. *Nonprofit Board Answer Book: A Practical Guide for Board Members and Chief Executives,* third ed. Washington, D.C.: Board Source, 2012.

Brawner, Lee B., and Donald K. Beck, Jr. *Determining Your Public Library's Future Size: A Needs Assessment & Planning Mode.* Chicago: American Library Association, 1996.

Buschman, John E. *Dismantling the Public Sphere: Situating and Sustaining Librarianship in the Age of the New Public Philosophy.* Westport, Conn.: Libraries Unlimited, 2003.

Greiner, Joy M. *Exemplary Public Libraries: Lessons in Leadership, Management, and Service.* Westport, Conn.: Libraries Unlimited, 2004.

Halstead, Deborah, Richard Jasper, and Felicia Little. *Disaster Planning: A How-to-Do-It Manual for Librarians.* New York: Neal-Schuman Publishers, 2005.

Illinois Library Association. *Serving Our Public 2.0: Standards for Illinois Public Libraries.* Chicago: Illinois Library Association, 2009.

Matthews, Joseph R. *Measuring for Results: The Dimensions of Public Library Effectiveness.* Westport, Conn.: Libraries Unlimited, 2004.

_____. *Preparing a Technology Plan.* Westport, Conn.: Libraries Unlimited, 2004.

Nelson, Sandra. *Implementing for Results: Your Strategic Plan in Action.* Chicago: Public Library Association, 2009.

_____. *Strategic Planning for Results,* Chicago: Public Library Association, 2008.

Yankey, John A. and Amy McClellan. *The Nonprofit Board's Role in Mission, Planning and Evaluation,* second ed. Washington, D.C.: Board Source, 2009.

Chapter 8

HUMAN RESOURCES

On par with a library's holdings are its human resources. Without appropriately trained staff, library resources would be inaccessible and useless to the community. Trustees on the library board hire and evaluate the library director, who has the major responsibility for library operations and oversight of library staff. The trustees, in turn, set policies to govern human resources issues affecting all staff.

The single most important decision a library board makes is to hire a library director. The success of the library's mission—its programs and services—depends upon the competence and commitment of that one professional more than any other factor.

Obtaining—and keeping—a successful library director must be a top priority for the library board. Along the same lines, the board must ensure that salary and benefits remain competitive, within the library's means. The familiar adage, "you get what you pay for," is as applicable to library management as to any other field requiring advanced education and high professional standards.

The issue of benefits looms especially large these days. With the health insurance industry in a state of high fluidity and under intense cost pressures, providing solid, satisfactory health coverage poses a major challenge to all employers. Moreover, Illinois requires that a retirement plan be provided for full-time municipal employees. Some plans may include some part-time staff as well. In addition, many employees wish to participate in tax deferred compensation programs that can be authorized by the library board as an attractive, virtually no-cost benefit. Library boards must take all these expectations into account when designing benefit plans.

Maintaining open, positive relations with staff also must be a high priority for library boards. Regular performance reviews for the library director, maintaining proper relations with subordinate staff, and handling grievances all fall under this broad umbrella.

> **Note: The Illinois Open Meeting Law, 5 ILCS 120, mandates that meetings of library boards be open to the public. However, the law does allow for closed meetings for discussion of sensitive topics such as interviewing of candidates, performance evaluations, hearing of grievances, and union negotiations. See the section, "Board Meetings the the Open Meetings Act," in Chapter 3 for the circumstances under which a closed meeting may be called.**

Hiring a Library Director

Before any recruiting begins, the library board must draft a comprehensive and accurate job description.

Job Description

The table on page 33 summarizes the type of information that a job description for library director should contain. The job description must be kept current, as it is the basis not only for hiring but also for performance evaluations.

Prioritizing Goals

Before recruiting begins, the board should revisit the long-range, strategic plan for the library. (See Chapter 7, "Planning.") What are the main goals in the plan? What activities do they emphasize? Perhaps a goal calls for expanding inadequate facilities. Or perhaps the library board has embraced a long-term objective of reaching out to a growing and underserved minority in the community.

Make a one-page bullet list to emphasize the major goals that the board has endorsed for future direction. This information will be useful in the recruiting process and in interviews.

Recruiting

For larger libraries, one of the most effective ways to advertise availability of a library director position is to place ads in professional journals such as the *Library Journal* and *American Libraries*. Joblines—online job-search resources—are also available and can be used effectively by libraries of all sizes. Both the ALA and the ILA websites have joblines. Regional library systems also post position vacancies on their websites, which draw a great number of local inquiries.

Joblines

Online Job-Search Resources

ALA	joblist.ala.org
ILA	http://www.ila.org
	Select Jobline

A job ad should include statistics indicating the scope of the job and salary information. A salary figure may be "ballparked" if the board wishes to leave room for negotiation. The ad might also highlight one or two major goals in the board's strategic plan for the library. The following is a sample job ad.

Legal Requirements

Library trustees, like other employers, must comply with state and federal laws that prohibit discrimination in hiring. It is illegal to discriminate on the basis of sex, race, creed, color, religion, age, country of national origin, individual lifestyle, or physical disability. If possible, have a legal advisor preview questions for and written communications to candidates.

Interviewing candidates

Interviewing is an art, as many people intuitively realize. There are library consulting firms that specialize in recruiting and advising institutions on effective and recommended recruitment practices. The process generally follows the steps below.

A library board should delegate interviewing tasks to a committee of the board. The same individuals should participate in all the interviews. Before any interview is conducted, the committee should draft a list of questions that will be asked of each interviewee. Some of the questions should pertain to the long-range goals that the board has previously identified.

The committee should provide time after each interview for interviewers to make written notes of their impressions.

The committee submits its recommendation to the whole board. Final candidates should meet with the full board, and if possible, with key staff members. When the board has reached consensus on a candidate, references should be checked. The job offer should specify salary and benefits along with the preferred starting date. There may be some flexibility involved, but a deadline should be clear. The other candidates should be notified of the selection only after the chosen candidate has accepted.

Job Title: Library Director

I. Job Responsibilities

Note: Depending on the size of the library, some of the duties may be delegated to the staff, but the responsibility for the successful completion of the work remains with the library director.

• Administrative role: Hire and supervise library staff; implement policies as established by the board; receive and expend funds according to budget; oversee services.

• General advisory role: Advise the board on issues from policymaking to budget preparation; inform the board about developments in the library field.

• Financial role: Prepare draft budget for consideration by the board; participate in presentation of the annual budget to municipal officials; prepare grant applications.

• Reportorial role: Prepare periodic budget reports and reports on circulation statistics or other relevant data; prepare annual report for ultimate submission to state library.

• Collection management role: Oversee selection of all materials; catalogue and process materials according to accepted standards; weed materials in accordance with policies established by the library board; advise the board on collection development issues.

• Facilities management role: Oversee maintenance of grounds and buildings; oversee custodial staff; oversee safety programs and state and federal regulations.

• Public relations role: Interface with community members and groups to develop support for the library; prepare publicity plans and handle media relations.

II. Qualities the Board is Seeking

• Excellent interpersonal skills, with the ability to facilitate discussion and build consensus.

• Excellent communications skills, including public speaking ability.

• Administrative skill, especially the ability to supervise staff and delegate responsibility, fairly and in accordance with board policies and state and federal laws.

• Ability to work well within lines of authority and to accept decisions made by the board.

• Excellent analytical skills. Ability to work with and manipulate statistical data.

• Ability to work with electronic media, including computers and the Internet.

• Ability to handle complaints and controversy with objectivity.

• Ability to plan and handle multiple, competing priorities, and accommodate deadlines.

III. Education and Experience

• Bachelor's degree; Master of Library Science degree preferred.

Performance Evaluations

Evaluation of the library director is an ongoing process, as is evaluation of the library's total offering of programs and services. The board should conduct such evaluations on at least an annual basis. The first such evaluation for a new director might occur at the end of a probationary period of several months.

The evaluation can be guided by a standard checklist of performance criteria. At least a couple of the performance criteria should be tied to goals in the library's long-range plan. The board and the library director should review the performance criteria at the beginning of the year so the basis of the future review is clear to all parties.

Setting Goals

No performance evaluation is complete without an eye to the future. The trustees and director should identify several objectives, based on goals in the long-range plan, for the director to work on in the coming months. These objectives then become inputs for future performance reviews.

Evaluation of the library director's performance should be based broadly on the following three factors.

Factors for Performance Evaluation

Job Description: Performance of the director as evaluated according to the written job description

Objectives: The director's progress carrying out previously identified objectives, in conjunction with specific long-range goals

Leadership: The success of the library in carrying out service programs, under the leadership of the director

Written Components

For reasons of consistency and legal viability, a formal performance evaluation should generate written records. These records should consist of

- a formal written evaluation by the board, signed by a representative of the board.
- a signed self-assessment submitted by the library director.

The written records are legal protection for both parties in the event that a disagreement involving the director's performance of duties should arise. They also provide a baseline for future performance evaluations.

Records Confidentiality

Human resources records require sensitive handling. Personal details of an employee's record are private and confidential in nature. Medical information is especially sensitive and should be kept separately from general personnel records. Management and use of human resources records are governed by the Personnel Record Review Act: 820 ILCS 40. For a sample personnel records request form, go to the Illinois State Library Administrative Ready Reference, http://www.webjunction.org/partners/Illinois/il-topics/readyref.html: select **Policy Model**. Then select **Personnel Policies;** select **Model Library Personnel Record Policy.**

Terminating Employment

For any number of reasons, the board and/or the director may decide that it is time for the director to go. Though the director may have been hired under contract, that contract may not be legally enforceable. If the director wants to resign, it is probably best for the board to accept that decision, even if there was a written or oral agreement about a longer period of employment.

If the board faces the delicate task of terminating the director's employment, it is highly advisable for the board to consult a legal advisor before firing a director. Illinois is an "at will employment" state, and most directors serve at the pleasure of the board. To avoid the possibility of litigation, a legal advisor will advise the board whether to document cause for termination of an employee or terminate the director "at will."

Whatever the cause of the parting, the board should conduct an exit interview with the director. A frank and open discussion of differences can identify problem areas that the board may want to remedy in future director relationships, or at the least, pitfalls to avoid in the next round of hiring.

Trustee Relationships with Subordinate Staff

The library board works directly with the library director in the administration of the library, and the director is directly answerable to the board. However, the situation with subordinate staff is quite different. These staff members will have been hired by the library director (past or present) and report directly to her or him. Therefore it is important that trustees avoid interference in the lines of authority between director and subordinate staff.

Occasionally, an aggrieved employee may approach a trustee with a complaint. The proper response on the trustee's part is to direct the employee to take up the problem with the library director.

The board should have a clearcut, written policy for handling staff grievances. If the problem cannot be solved at the director's level, then it may have to come before the board—but only according to an established, written policy.

For a sample grievance policy, go to the Illinois State Library Administrative Ready Reference: http://www.webjunction.org/partners/illinois/il-topics/readyref.html: select **Policy Model.** Then select **Personnel Policies;** select **Grievance Procedure Policy.**

Salary and Benefits

Determining appropriate salary levels involves two hard realities of economics: available resources and supply-and-demand competition among the available pool of personnel. To attract good people, the board of trustees should offer a competitive salary for the range of duties each position entails. The board sets the compensation structures and the level of each job with a minimum and maximum salary for the position; the director administers the salary and benefit program for the other employees, according to the board's policies. The board confirms new hires and salaries.

The Illinois Library Association advocates fair compensation for library employees within these guidelines:

- A qualified, entry-level librarian should be compensated at no less than the same rate as an entry-level public school teacher with a master's degree, with adjustment to reflect a librarian's 12-month (rather than teacher's 10-month) work year.
- All other library staff should be compensated at levels that are competitive with salaries paid for equivalent positions in other public agencies within the same or approximately the same service area.

For additional help in setting appropriate salary for staff positions:
- confer with other comparable libraries in your library system or region and other local governmental agencies.
- seek input from other libraries of similar size, from school districts, or from the municipality.

Benefits are becoming an ever bigger part of the total rewards package. The cost of health insurance continues to rise at rates far ahead of annual inflation. If possible, the board should consult with a benefits specialist to find the best, most cost-effective combination of benefits. Some certified public accountants (CPA's) now offer benefits consulting as part of their services. Also seek options to join cooperatives to get good benefits at a more competitive price.

Human Resources Policy Manual

A necessary tool for employer and employees alike is a human resources policy manual. Such a manual might be prepared and maintained by a board committee in close consultation with the library director.

Document salary grades, benefits, paid holidays, vacation, and any other information relevant to staff in the manual. Distribute the manual to all staff members and have them sign a statement indicating that they received a copy. The manual is a guide to the policies of the library. Do not consider it or imply that it is a contract.

Union Negotiations

Public employees in Illinois have the right to join unions to bargain collectively for salary, benefits, and working conditions. In libraries in which staff members are unionized, it is the board's responsibility to negotiate terms of employment with union representatives. The library director should, of course, have input to these negotiations. In the final event, however, it is the board that will have to reach agreement in collective bargaining.

It is critically important that trustees adhere to state and federal laws governing labor relations when negotiating with union representatives. It is equally important that the board observe legally proper conduct during union organization and election activities.

It is highly recommended that the board may consult with an attorney with expertise in labor relations. The following resources may also be useful.

National Labor Relations Board: http://www.nlrb.gov/
American Arbitration Association: http://www.adr.org

Resources

Baldwin, David A. *The Library Compensation Handbook: A Guide for Administrators, Librarians and Staff.* Westport, Conn.: Libraries Unlimited, 2003.

Cole, Jack and Suzanne Mahmoodi. *Selecting a Library Director: A Workbook for Members of a Selection Committee,* revised 1998. St. Paul, Minn.: Friends of the Library Development and Services, the Minnesota State Library Agency, a unit of the Minnesota Department of Education, 1998.

Cravey, Pamela. *Protecting Library Staff, Users, Collections and Facilities: A How-to-Do-It Manual.* New York: Neal-Schuman Publishers, 2001.

Evans, G. Edward. *Performance Management and Appraisal: A How-To-Do-it Manual for Trustees and Librarians.* New York: Neal-Schuman Publishers, 2004.

Chapter 9

FACILITIES

A public library serves people of all ages, widely varied educational experience, and multiple linguistic backgrounds. It endeavors to meet educational and cultural needs of these diverse communities against a backdrop of rapid and continual technological change. No wonder libraries and the facilities that house them tend to become mismatched over time. Consider any of the following scenarios in a public library. Do any sound familiar?

An Ill-fitting Suit . . .

- The library director has just catalogued and processed a major publisher's new eight-volume series of books on global warming and climate change. When library staff members attempt to shelve this timely and valuable source in the appropriate number range in the reference stacks, there is no room for shifting books on the shelves to accommodate the series. The director and staff now have to come up with a makeshift solution to their space problem.
- The local community has experienced something of a "baby boom" within the last decade; as a result, the Saturday story hour for children is popular as never before. Two years ago, the library split the 11 A.M. Saturday story hour into two story hours on Saturday, at 11 A.M. and 2 P.M. Now, both of the children's story sessions are overcrowded.
- Because of space and wiring limitations, the library can accommodate only two online catalogue computer terminals. Five years ago, that level of support was adequate. Now, at high-use times, patrons have to take a number and wait in line to use the computerized card catalogue.
- When the library was built in 1914, large floor-to-ceiling windows were incorporated into the design to provide ample natural lighting in the main reading room. Then in the 1970s, the cost of energy and the cost of replacing large, custom panes of glass convinced the library board of that era to close up most of the window space and install small, standard-sized windows. Ever since, patrons have complained about the dark gloom in the reading room and the eerie, unpleasant shadows cast by the fluorescent lighting.

A Cautionary Tale

In the 1970s, the main library of the Chicago Public Library was moved out of its long-time, 1897 Beaux-Arts home, which the city then transformed into a downtown cultural center. The library was temporarily housed in the Mandel

Building on Chicago's major commercial thoroughfare, Michigan Avenue. The library's holdings were scattered among several floors, challenging and confusing staff and patrons alike. Many users of the main library remember the 1970s as a frustrating era of misshelved or missing books. In 1982, the city moved the main library to occupy the recently vacated Goldblatt department store on the city's traditional Loop shopping street, State Street—another temporary and less than ideal arrangement.

Through careful planning with the city and a re-assessment of user needs, this story does have a happy ending. In 1991, Chicago dedicated the magnificent Harold Washington Library Center. The structure fittingly hosts the main collection of the nation's "second city" and lends a dignified, stable presence to Chicago's South Loop area.

In Chapter 7, "Planning," you read about the importance of long-range, or strategic, library planning. Adept, timely planning may enable you to avoid unhappy scenarios such as those described above. Conversely, inadequate planning will surely land you sooner or later in one unhappy scenario or another (or many).

An important part of the library board's duties is providing and maintaining physical facilities. This responsibility involves monitoring existing facilities and—when necessary and appropriate—planning and budgeting for renovation or construction of facilities.

Evaluating Library Facilities

Staying one step ahead of the forces at work in our contemporary world challenges the most meticulous and thoughtful of planners. Demographic shifts alter communities; technological change renders yesterday's practices and procedures obsolete.

To stay on top of things, a board of trustees must keep a finger on the pulse of the library and community. One good way to do this, of course, is to solicit staff, patron, and community feedback, and to incorporate such feedback into the library's strategic planning. Another way to "take the pulse" is to conduct an annual evaluation of library facilities, possibly with the help of a professional library building consultant. The consultant is typically an experienced librarian who has extensive experience planning and implementing library building projects. At the heart of the planning process are the following questions:

- What are our users' needs?
- What services are we offering to meet those needs? What needs are we not meeting?
- Do our library facilities adequately support library services?

The final question, about facilities, is closely related to the first three. If trustees, library director, and staff find they cannot provide services to meet community needs in existing physical facilities, then facility changes of one kind or another will be necessary.

Evaluating physical space can become quite technical. Knowledge about library design and ergonomics (how space and facilities can be maximized for safe, efficient use by the human body) is critically important. As finances and professional availability allow, libraries are well advised to engage the services of a building consultant for facilities evaluation, especially if a building program appears to be in the offing.

Another online resource for library consultants is LibraryConsultants.org at http://www.library-consultants. org.

Of course, the library director and staff will have major parts to play in any evaluation of library facilities, as they observe the daily use patterns of patrons and are aware of inadequacies that reoccur.

Precise metrics for determining library space needs are available in Appendix L of *Serving Our Public 2.0.* To obtain an electronic copy of this document go online to the Illinois State Library Administrative Ready Reference, http://www.webjunction.org/partners/Illinois/il-topics/readyref.html: select **Serving Our Public**.

Library Facility Evaluation Guidelines . . .

- Conformance to state and federal laws regarding access by persons with disabilities, particularly the Americans with Disabilities Act (ADA)
- ADA became federal law in 1990. ADA establishes specific building codes to ensure accessibility for disabled people.
- For more information, access "ADA Accessibility Guidelines for Buildings and Facilities" at the following federal government-sponsored website: www.access-board.gov/adaag/html/adaag.htm.
- Shelving space

  A board-established policy of "weeding out" old materials should clear the way for new materials. However, if new exceeds old, library staff will face a shelving crunch and solutions will be needed.
- Adequacy of display furniture

  Display furniture such as periodical or paperback racks take up floor space, but are important inclusions to store materials appropriately and attract patrons' interest.
- Staff usage areas

  Staff members need adequate working space. A computer workstation and adequate desk and file space are the minimal requirements. Staff also need amenities such as a break area with table and chairs.
- Facilities for technology support

  At minimum, a library needs computer terminal(s) for online card catalogue access, computer(s) for Internet access, photocopier(s), telephones, and fax machine(s); and adequate wiring support for all equipment requirements. Moreover, many patrons regard electrical outlets for their laptop computers as a necessity.
- Lighting

  Adequate artificial lighting is critical for use of materials as well as vision health. Additionally, natural light enhances the library environment aesthetically. Natural light must not, however, be strongly intrusive, as in direct morning or afternoon sunlight, especially in areas where computers will be in use.
- Circulation/checkout areas

  Counter space should be adequate to accommodate the flow of patrons. The checkout desk must have at least one station to accommodate wheelchair height, according to ADA regulations. This station will also be at a friendly height for young children.
- Reference

  If possible, a separate service point should be created for patrons to interact with the reference librarian. A study area, preferably with computers offering Internet access, should be in proximity of the reference librarian so personal assistance can be readily provided.
- Children's Services

  A separate area should be created for children that reflects their special interests, accommodates their collections, and allows for their youthful chatter. Staff assistance should be nearby to help children and parents in selecting age-appropriate materials. The space should accommodate school visits and programs, if possible.
- Meeting Room

  Although not all facilities can provide a space for library programs and community groups, it should be a goal for planning. The library can enhance its value to the community by providing programs of interest to children and adults. By offering a meeting place to civic groups, the library will become the "heart of the community" and a relevant resource in people's lives.

- Storage, Mechanical Equipment and Maintenance Areas

  A surprising amount of space is required for non-public service functions in a library. Storage is needed for supplies used in ordering and processing, for required retention of records, and for materials awaiting cataloguing or repair. Cleaning supplies and equipment must be stored safely, and convenient access to a "janitor's closet" with sink is essential for maintenance activities. Areas for heating and cooling equipment should be located in safe areas with attention given to the impact of noise of operation on the library service areas and neighbors.

- Special service areas

  If space is available, some libraries provide a quiet study room, a business resources room, or a local history room. Allocation of special spaces is determined by local needs and building layouts.

- Amenities

  Restrooms and water fountains must be clean and accessible to everyone, including the disabled. The number and/or size of bathrooms should accommodate patrons at all times without imposing long waits. Local zoning codes should be consulted.

- Climate control

  The library should provide a comfortable environment year-round. Heating and cooling systems must be clean and safe to protect against buildup of molds, bacteria, or other pathogens. The library should retain the regular services of a reputable heating/AC (HVAC) company.

- Cleaning service

  The importance of maintaining a clean environment has been highlighted in recent years by press stories about possible links between rising asthma rates in children and the dusty environments in which many children live. Library officials should continually monitor the adequacy of cleaning the library, whether done by janitorial staff or a service.

- General appearance and condition of building(s)

  The trustees should be alert to any evidence of possible structural problems. Where concerns arise, a structural engineer should be retained to make appropriate inspections. Facilities that look dated or shabby may turn away patrons: is it time for a major redecoration? An engineer can also prepare a schedule for structural maintenance (tuckpointing, window re-sealing, etc.) and systems maintenance (HVAC, electrical, etc.) for planning and budgeting purposes.

- Security

  The library should have adequate protection during off-hours, such as an appropriately alarmed and monitored security system. Security staff may also be needed to assure a safe, positive environment for patrons and staff when the library is open. The library might choose to hire an on-site security guard during certain hours, particularly in busy periods and closing hours.

- Protection against fire

  Most municipalities have fire codes. Library trustees should verify that library facilities meet all such codes. In particular, care should be taken with flammable materials, and fire extinguishers and alarms should be installed according to code. Emergency exits should be well-marked and lit. Staff should have an evacuation plan and a storm "take-over" plan and practice it from time to time.

- Location in community

  Towns, cities, and communities change. Is the library still in a central, reasonably accessible location for the whole community? If not, should branch outlets or mobile service be considered?

- Parking

Fifty years ago, far fewer people drove cars in their daily activities than today. Patrons expect to be able to drive to the library and park; otherwise, many will opt for some other activity. Verify that parking is adequate for the library hours of greatest use. Verify that disabled parking spaces are provided, in accordance with ADA regulations. There may be local guidelines or zoning codes regarding the number of parking spaces needed.

What Next?

A thorough, annual facilities evaluation might lead the trustees to any of several conclusions. For example, finding facilities to be adequate might lead them to identify a few minor improvements to be made. On the other hand, the trustees might identify major shortcomings in the facilities that can be remedied only by a building program. That program might take the shape of an expansion of existing facilities or the construction of an entirely new library.

Deciding To Build

A building program is a long, complex process. The potential payoff for the library's mission and future is huge, but the potential pitfalls are numerous.

A Building Committee

When trustees have concluded that fulfilling the library's mission in the community calls for new facilities, the board should form a building committee. This committee should embrace at least some of the trustees, members of the community, and the library director.

In the early stages, this committee might be called a Building Study Committee to reflect its pre-commitment function. Once an architect has been hired, plans have been approved, and a contractor has been hired, the committee might evolve into a Construction Committee.

Library Building Program Statement

A building committee's first major task is to draft a building program statement. This is a carefully written document that describes the general building requirements necessary to satisfy the library's functional needs (which, of course, should be based on community service needs identified in the library's strategic plan). Library building consultants can be very helpful with this process and may be required for library construction grants.

The building program statement will answer four questions, elaborating in considerable detail:
- What are the library's overall space needs?
- How should the space be broken down into departments or service areas?
- How should these areas relate to one another?
- What furniture and equipment will be needed in each area to function efficiently and respond to user needs?

The building committee will use the building program statement as a checklist for evaluating plans submitted by an architect later in the life of the project. A well-written building program statement will help ensure that the architect "gets it right" and should minimize or avoid disputes and confusion among the committee members about "what we decided on."

Hiring an Architect

Once the trustees have made a clear commitment to building and have prepared a building program statement, the board's next step will be to engage the services of an architect. A good way to approach this critically important task is to visit libraries that have recently completed building programs. Also see the "Resources" section at the end of this chapter.

The board should solicit presentations by several architects. Each candidate should be interviewed and examples of his or her work on similar projects should be reviewed. Establishing a harmonious working relationship between architect and building committee members is critically important.

When the board has made its selection, the architect and board will work out a formal written contract. The board will want to make provisions for attorney review of the contract.

Additionally, the board may need to include a contingency provision in the contract to allow for the outcome of a public referendum, if such is required. If the referendum fails, how will the architect be compensated? How can the board limit its financial outlay to accommodate this unwished-for outcome?

Funding a Building Program

Library funding comes from several sources. The following sections detail funding sources that may be available for a building program.

Levies

The Illinois Local Library Act establishes that governmental units such as cities, towns, and villages that maintain public libraries may decide, by referendum, to levy 0.02 percent of property taxes for construction projects in addition to taxes allocated for support of libraries. (See 75 ILCS 5/3-1.)

Likewise, library districts may levy 0.02 percent of property taxes for construction projects. The additional levy requires a referendum if the requisite percentage of voters in the district petition for one. (See 75 ILCS 16/35-5.)

Bond Issues

Municipalities or library districts may issue bonds to fund construction programs. A bond issue requires voter approval in a referendum.

- For information about bond issues for libraries in municipalities, see 75 ILCS 5/5; 75 ILCS 35.
- For information about bond issues in library districts, see 75 ILCS 16/40-10, 15, 20.

There are financial consultants available to help estimate costs and plan for a referendum.

Grants

State construction grants may be available through the Illinois State Library. For information on such grants, go online to the Illinois State Library Administrative Ready Reference: http://www.webjunction.org/partners/illinois/il-topics/readyref.html: select **Planning for Grants.**

Additionally, there are many opportunities available through national and local governmental agencies, not-for-profit organizations, foundations, and professional associations.

Resources

Cravey, Pamela. *Protecting Library Staff, Users, Collections and Facilities: A How-to-Do-It Manual.* New York: Neal-Schuman Publishers, 2001.

McCabe, Gerard B., and James R. Kennedy, eds. *Planning the Modern Public Library Building.* Westport, Conn.: Greenwood, 2003.

Sannwald, William W. *Checklist of Library Building Design Considerations,* fifth ed. Chicago: American Library Association, 2008.

Woodward, Jeannette. *Countdown to a New Library: Managing the Building Project,* second ed. Chicago: American Library Association, 2010.

Chapter 10

BUDGETING AND FINANCIAL MANAGEMENT

Most people understand the basic logic of budgeting: you take in money, called income or revenue; and you spend money, called expenditure, to obtain goods and services. In a healthy, well-regulated economy—whether a home, business, or government—expenditure does not exceed income.

A public library is largely dependent on the governing authority for its tax support, whether the governing authority is the host municipality or township, or in the case of library districts, the revenue generating taxing authority of the district itself. No less than other economies, the budgetary and financial health of a public library relies on the basic budgetary logic of revenue and expenditures.

Within budgetary constraints, library officials seek adequate revenues; authorize appropriate expenditures; and keep careful track of money flow. These activities are all part of a program of financial management.

Income for Public Libraries

Most of the income for public libraries comes from taxation on the part of the governing authority. For most Illinois public libraries, that authority is a city, town, village, county, or township. In district libraries, the library district is itself the taxing authority.

Revenue from Property Taxes

The primary source of revenue for most public libraries in Illinois is local property taxes. The Illinois Local Library Act establishes that governmental units such as cities, towns, and villages that maintain public libraries will allocate 0.15 percent of property taxes to funding of those libraries. Communities may choose by referendum to raise the library tax rate to any percentage up to and including 0.60 percent.

Additionally, communities may decide, by referendum, to levy an additional 0.02 percent "maintenance levy" for maintenance, repairs, and alterations of library buildings and equipment.

Library districts may levy the same tax rates as the municipal libraries. The only difference is that a district library is its own taxing authority. Library districts receive their taxes directly from the county. In the case of a home rule municipality that hosts its municipal library, the library may be given the same power to levy.

In recent years, some Illinois counties, including Cook County and the Chicago metropolitan "collar" counties have adopted so-call "tax caps," more properly called the Property Tax Extension Limitation Law (PTELL) 35 ILCS 200/18-185. This law constrains the rate of growth in property tax collection in neighborhoods where property values are rising rapidly. As a result of PTELL, revenues available to public libraries in some locales are growing at a slower rate than formerly. For some libraries, revenues are actually decreasing due to the implementation of PTELL.

For more information, see http://www.ila.org/advocacy/tax-cap-information.

All of this becomes relevant and important when the time comes to estimate revenue in a budgeting cycle. To obtain reasonably reliable revenue projections, library trustees should work with municipal finance officers.

Supplemental Taxes

Public libraries are eligible to levy several additional taxes. These additional taxes are usually referred to as supplemental or special taxes. The special taxes provide additional funding sources for the costs of items such as insurance, Social Security, Illinois Municipal Retirement Fund (IMRF), building/maintenance, and risk management. For those libraries located in a Property Tax Extension Limitation Law (PTELL) county, sometimes known as a property tax county, some special taxes may require a referendum. Contact the county clerk to determine if the ordinances may be levied with or without a referendum.

The following list indicates types of taxes and the applicable citation:

General Corporate (Library)
75 ILCS 5/3-1 for municipal libraries; 75 ILCS 16/35-10 for district libraries

Building & Maintenance
75 ILCS 5/3-1 for municipal libraries; 75 ILCS 16/35-5 for district libraries

Tort & Immunity (Insurance) Fund
745 ILCS 10/9-107 for municipal and district libraries; also see 75 ILCS 5/4-14

Audit
65 ILCS 5/8-8-8 for municipal and district libraries

Illinois Municipal Retirement Fund (IMRF)
40 ILCS 5/7-171 for municipal and district libraries

Social Security
40 ILCS 5/21-110 and 21-110.1 for municipal and district libraries

Medicare
40 ILCS 5/21-110 and 21-110.1 for municipal and district libraries

Working Cash Fund
75 ILCS 5/3-9 and 75 ILCS 5/4-13 for municipal libraries; 75 ILCS 16/35-35 &16/30-95 for district libraries

Special Reserve Fund
75 ILCS 5/5-8 for municipal libraries; 75 ILCS 16/40-50 & 16/40-5 for district libraries

State Grants and Federal LSTA Grants

In addition to taxes, a number of state and federal grants are available to public libraries as potential revenue streams. In Illinois, most of these grants are administered through the Illinois State Library in Springfield.

The U.S. Congress allocates federal grants to public libraries through the Library Services and Technology Act (LSTA). This federal source of funding has been available in one form or another since 1956. In Illinois, public libraries apply for LSTA through the Illinois State Library.

Soliciting grants requires special skills and thorough knowledge of the grant application process. The library director or other staff member who is experienced in applying for grants should prepare and submit all grant applications.

To apply for federal or state grants, visit the website of the Illinois State Library. A good place to start is the Administrative Ready Reference, http://www.webjunction.org/partners/illinois/il-topics/readyref.html: select **Planning for Grants**.

Grants from Other Organizations

There are many opportunities available through national, state, and local governmental agencies, not-for-profit organizations, and foundations, in addition to professional associations.

E-rate Funding from the Federal Government

The U.S. Congress passed legislation in 1996 to help public libraries cope with financial demands of the technological revolution, such as buying computers and leasing Internet service. The legislation set up the so-called "e-fund." According to provisions in the law, the e-fund is funded by a special federal tax on phone companies. The Federal Communications Commission (FCC) is charged with accepting applications for e-fund grants, approving grants, and distributing the money through the School and Library Division. More information on the application process can be obtained from the Universal Service Administrative Company website, www.sl.universalservice.org.

Note that acceptance of e-fund grants requires libraries to adhere to certain federal regulations. Public libraries must install and maintain filtering software on computers that support Internet connections, in compliance with the Children's Internet Protection Act (CIPA), passed by Congress in 2000. For more information on CIPA, see Chapter 6, "Intellectual Freedom."

Charitable Donations

Public libraries encourage charitable donations from private citizens and companies. (This topic is discussed in more detail in Chapter 11, "Fundraising.")

Public libraries may receive tax exempt charitable gifts in their role as part of a municipality or as a sovereign political subdivision (in the case of district libraries). Any such donation vests in the library board of trustees. The board of trustees automatically becomes a special trustee of the donated property. No special incorporation is required.

Another way in which a library may choose to accept charitable gifts is to set up a tax exempt foundation under Internal Revenue Service Code §501(c)(3). This approach has inherent costs, such as incorporation fees and accountant fees for preparing federal tax returns. Some libraries may find the foundation structure helpful in conducting development campaigns.

For more details about accepting charitable donations as a public library, go online to the Administrative Ready Reference (previously cited): select **Charitable Giving**.

Library Expenditures

As we all know, everything costs. The services that a public library provides require staff, facilities, resources, and many other costly inputs. The following list summarizes the main categories of expenditures for a typical public library.

Library Expenditures

- Staff salaries and benefits
  - Because libraries are service-driven organizations, expenses associated with obtaining and keeping competent, qualified staff will be the largest entry in the accounts ledger.
- Materials
  - Books, e-books, DVDs, audio books, and periodicals are all examples of library materials.
- Operations
  - This category includes building maintenance, utilities, supplies used by staff and patrons, and many other items.
- Technology
  - All the computers, scanners, printers, photocopiers, Internet connections, regional database connections, local area networks, and telecommunications fall into this category. Of course, technology needs are continually growing and changing and require frequent reinvesting to upgrade and improve services.
- Additionally, public libraries may have special, significant expenditures at particular times, such as expenditures associated with building a new library structure.

The Budgeting Process

Budgeting is a complex, collaborative process. It requires many different inputs and achieves best results when many voices expressing various viewpoints are heard. A budget should reflect the appropriate mix of visionary creativity and well informed fiscal reality.

In the broadest sense, two inputs are required to fashion a budget: (1) a needs and goals assessment, and (2) an estimate of available resources.

The needs and goals assessment comes directly from the library board's long-range plan. Planning and budgeting go hand-in-hand. "The budget is the long-range plan in numbers, and the long-range plan is the budget in words," as some library administrators have observed.

Lines of Responsibility

Although budgeting is a collaborative responsibility, ultimately the library board must put its stamp of approval on a budget and submit it to the governing (funding) authority. (Note that the ultimate funding authority in a library district is the library board itself. These comments apply to municipal libraries.)

The board has ultimate responsibility for the budget. However, trustees will not be able to do this job without significant input from staff, especially the library director.

The director, in turn, will probably depend upon other staff to help collect pertinent data and assess library needs. All these players should have a say.

Finally, the governing authority gives a thumbs up or down on budget matters, based on their understanding of community needs and interests.

Steps in the Budgeting Process

Budgeting is an ongoing activity in library management. The following list is intended only to suggest the broadest outline of the budgeting process.

Budgeting Guidelines . . .

- Begin well in advance of deadlines.
- Evaluate last year's budget. Ask: How well did it support services? How well did it enable library staff and trustees to carry out long-range plans?
- Consider salaries and benefits early in the process; these costs will rank among the highest in the budget. (See the "Library Expenditures" list earlier in this chapter.)

- Continually evaluate budget decisions in light of goals and objectives established during the planning process. (See Chapter 7, "Planning.")
- Earmark annually, if possible, a sum for a new program or service enhancement.
- Try to anticipate next year's problem areas and obtain preliminary estimates.
- Develop a multi-year plan to fund building and equipment repairs and replacement. Proactive planning will significantly reduce costly, unbudgeted capital expenses.
- Don't try to hide the budget: work to obtain staff and community buy-in.
- When the board has approved the budget, prepare to make a professional presentation to the appropriate funding authorities. Be prepared to explain and justify costs to municipal officials. Persuade authorities that they have a stake in the library's success in the community.

Financial Management of the Library

In general terms, financial management is all the things a library board, director, and staff members do to implement the budget. It is an ongoing daily, weekly, and monthly task.

Funds must be dispersed and collected continually to keep a public library running. State statutes and library board bylaws specify procedures for making purchases and dispersing funds. For example, a provision in the bylaws may grant the treasurer of the board check-writing privileges for expenses up to a certain amount; it may require joint signatures of both the treasurer and the board president for large expenses.

Typically a public library has an operating fund, out of which ongoing, regular expenses are paid. Additionally, libraries may have a capital fund and, perhaps an endowment fund. The following table summarizes types of library funds.

Types of Library Funds

Fund	Purpose
Operating	To pay day-to-day expenses and deposit regular sources of income
Capital	To pay for special, large expenses such as for a building program, major equipment purchase, or structural improvements
Endowment	May be established to receive and invest monetary charitable donations
Working Cash	Enables libraries to have in its funds, at all times, sufficient money to meet demands for ordinary and necessary and committed expenditures for library purposes. (75 ILCS 5/3-9 and 5/4-13; for district libraries, 75 ILCS 16/30-95 and 16/35-35)

Periodic Reports and Audits

Tracking the collection and dispersal of funds on a regular, rational basis is critically important. Personnel should file with the board regular financial reports reflecting standard accounting practices. Such reports might be generated by the library director or the director in collaboration with the board treasurer, for example. Reports might be presented on a quarterly basis for smaller operations, or on a monthly basis for larger libraries. Financial reports should be organized in useful categories with sufficient information to monitor expenses. Categories generally include:

- Salaries
- Benefit costs
- Commodities (supplies)
- Contractual expenses

- Capital expenses

More descriptive account lines may be added to each category to track expenses.

Public libraries in Illinois are required by law to submit an annual report to the principal funding agency (village, township, city, or library district) and to submit a duplicate copy to the Illinois State Library.

Public libraries are also advised to contract with a qualified professional to conduct an annual audit. Municipal public libraries with income of $850,000 or greater are required by law in Illinois to conduct an annual audit. District libraries must submit a comptroller's report even if they do not conduct an audit. These mandated records are public documents that must be retained and made available to the public.

Resources

The Illinois State Library's Administrative Ready Reference Menu (previously cited) offers several resources related to budgeting and financial management of a public library. The following items may be especially useful:

- Charitable Giving
  - General guidelines and samples of letters to donors
- Non-Resident Fee Calculation
  - A formula for calculating library fees to charge non-residents
- Ordinances
  - Under "Financial" subhead: Illinois laws concerning financial aspects of library management
- Planning for Grants
  - Information about grants available to public libraries through the Illinois State Library
- Policy Model
  - Under "Financial" subhead: coverage on topics including budget and finance policy; division of financial responsibilities between the board and the library director; and investment of public funds
- Property Tax Extension Limitation Law (PTELL)
  - Details about PTELL, popularly known as "tax caps" (See the subsection, "Revenue from Property Taxes," near the beginning of this chapter.)

Specific Titles

Berger, Steven. *Understanding Nonprofit Financial Statements,* third ed. Washington, D.C.: Board Source, 2008.

Diamond, Stewart H. and W. Britt Isaly. *Financial Manual for Illinois Public Libraries.* Chicago: Illinois Library Association, 2007.

Fry, Robert P. *Minding the Money: An Investment Guide for Nonprofit Board Members.* Washington, D.C.: Board Source, 2004.

Lang, Andrew S. *Financial Responsibilities of Nonprofit Boards,* second ed. Washington, D.C.: Board Source, 2009.

Prentice, Ann E. *Financial Planning for Libraries,* second ed. Lanham, Md.: Scarecrow Press, 1996.

Chapter 11

FUNDRAISING

The bulk of funding for public libraries in our communities comes from local property tax revenue. This is as it should be; public libraries are truly people's institutions, administered for the benefit of the local community and its residents.

Today, many local and state governments face mounting financial pressures, to which they often respond by curtailing the annual growth of public funding. Now more than ever, it is important for libraries to seek additional sources of funding through grants and fundraising campaigns.

For libraries experiencing financial limitations, library administrators should pursue relevant grant opportunities aggressively. For information about accessing federal and state grant money, see Chapter 10, "Budgeting and Financial Management."

Library trustees and staff should also consider fundraising options when the need to supplement standard appropriations looms large.

To Incorporate or Not?

In Chapter 10, "Budgeting and Financial Management," you read that a public library can receive charitable donations in its role as a sovereign political entity or part thereof. Donations vest in the library board of trustees, and the board becomes the special trustee of the donated property. No special legal steps or fees are required to raise funds on this basis.

Many libraries, however, find that they have strong incentives to set up a tax-exempt charitable foundation under Internal Revenue Service (IRS) Code §501(c)(3). Many donors, especially corporations and foundations, give only to IRS-qualified foundations to ensure the tax-deductible status of their contributions. Moreover, corporations offer employee matching-gift programs only to 501(c)(3) or similar incorporations. Because a foundation is permanent, its existence may encourage planned, annual giving as well as memorial or other bequests.

The downsides of the 501(c)(3) foundation are that the library must:

- allocate startup funds for fees related to setting up a foundation, including attorney fees, incorporation fees, and other costs.
- budget annual costs related to the foundation, such as attorney fees and preparation fees for tax returns and annual reports.
- provide staff to administer foundation activities as well as space dedicated to foundation

operations.

An Alternative: The Fund for Illinois Libraries

For small libraries, the costs related to foundation incorporation may be too large to justify the foundation approach to fundraising. Similarly, libraries whose fundraising needs are largely focused on a one-time project such as a building program may not wish to incur the overhead of incorporating. Such libraries may be able to take an alternative approach by using the Fund for Illinois Libraries.

The Fund for Illinois Libraries, a 501(c)(3) foundation, was created to serve as a clearing-house for corporations or individuals wishing to make donations only to tax-exempt foundations. Administered by the Illinois Library Association (ILA), the fund will process the original donation and issue a check to the library that the donor wishes to have the money. For more information, go online to http://www.ila.org/fund.

The Charitable Foundation

When the library board concludes that setting up a charitable foundation is in its best interests, the board is well advised to consult an attorney or CPA who has experience with tax-exempt foundations.

Additionally, a detailed description of the incorporation process is available online at the Illinois State Library Administrative Ready Reference, http://www.webjunction.org/partners/illinois/il-topics/readyref.html: select **Charitable Giving**. Then select **Steps in Organizing a Not-for-Profit Corporation**.

A Board of Directors

A tax-exempt foundation is administered by its own board of directors. Choosing the individuals to serve on this board is critically important to the ultimate success of fundraising activities. This selection task typically falls to the library board of trustees.

Each candidate for membership on the foundation board of directors should be a responsible community member who is familiar with the role of the public library in the community and is willing to devote time to his or her foundation involvement. Foundation board members control investment of donated funds, so at least some of the members should have solid financial experience. Members should also have strong connections in the community so they bring a base of contacts for potential donors.

Fundraising Campaigns

As a trustee of a public library, one of your primary responsibilities is to advocate for resources that the library needs to carry out its mission. In other chapters of this book, you have considered how to go about negotiating budgets with municipal officials or how to request state or federal grants. Your fiduciary role as trustee may also require you to go among your neighbors in the community to ask for money.

The library director shares fundraising responsibilities with members of the library board. Obviously board members and the director will want to coordinate their fundraising activities.

Small or mid-sized libraries will probably do best to dispense with the services of professional fundraisers. Donors may prove more generous if they feel that all their giving goes directly to support the library. On the other hand, a large library may need to rely on professional services.

As with other endeavors, fundraising requires careful, thoughtful planning. The way in which you and other library officials approach the community "with hat in hand" could make a big difference in the ultimate results of a fundraising campaign. The following list summarizes points for conducting a successful fundraising campaign.

Tips for Successful Fundraising . . .

- Identify a specific monetary need. Develop a convincing justification for the need, and state it clearly and succinctly.
- Set and publicize a monetary goal for the campaign; the figure chosen should be feasible within the community's means.
- Budget costs for the fundraising campaign; these are likely to include publicity materials, media time for publicity, and perhaps personnel.
- Set up a campaign timetable with specific monetary goals aligned to specific "mileposts."
- Work to identify potential donors within the community. If possible, elicit commitments for significant contributions before publicizing the campaign. The campaign can then kick off with the announcement of "leading donors."
- Seek endorsements from community leaders.
- Carefully assign responsibilities for all aspects of the campaign; solicit volunteer support to as full an extent as possible.
- Develop attractive, interesting brochures, posters, gift cards, mailings, and other materials to publicize and implement the campaign.
- Plan exhibits in prominent public places.
- Implement an effective public relations campaign in community media before and during the campaign.
- Don't extend fundraising beyond the stated end date; it is more effective to start up a new campaign later than to break faith with the public by extending the end date.

From the Donors' Point of View

People's motivations for giving to charitable causes vary widely, but nearly all donors expect a few modest benefits in return. Most donors expect to receive some kind of acknowledgment of their gift. They want to feel assured that the money will be used for designated purposes and not be used up by incidental costs such as fundraisers' fees. They want to have confidence in the competence and propriety of the charitable organization's managers. And donors want to receive the maximum tax advantages allowed by law for their donations.

By considering fundraising activities from the donors' point of view, you and your fellow fundraisers on the board of trustees and the staff can maximize the appeal of a fund drive to potential donors. Put simply, you want your donors to feel great about the act of giving—so they will give and give again.

The following list identifies positive ways to communicate with your potential donor base in the community during a fundraising campaign.

Fundraising with Donors in Mind . . .

- Provide a clear statement of the goals of the campaign and what the library intends to use the money for.
- Publicize a positive, appealing message, rather than a negative message accompanied by scare tactics or prophecies of doom.
- Accept "no" as an answer; many people dislike being harassed by fundraisers and some will turn against even a worthy organization if it uses overly aggressive solicitation tactics.
- Be prepared to provide up-to-date financial reports of the library upon request.
- Be prepared to identify the board of trustees and library director upon request.
- Assure donors that their contribution will be treated confidentially and that data about them will not be given or sold to other organizations.
- Give donors the opportunity to use the widest possible variety of payment methods;

accept pledges to pay within a specific period of time. Allocate staff to follow up on unpaid pledges, and build a 10-percent nonpayment rate into your financial calculations.
- Acknowledge every gift with a personalized "thank-you" letter, clearly stating the tax deductibility status of the gift.

Friends of the Library and Fundraising

Many public libraries are fortunate to have the support of a Friends of the Library organization. The range of activities of most Friends' groups can vary, but they are often focused on fundraising activities such as book sales, bake sales, or membership dues. To encourage donations, some Friends groups have established themselves as tax-exempt charitable foundations and have become very successful fundraising auxiliaries for the library. For best results, Friends, trustees, and the library director should carefully coordinate fundraising activities.

Resources

Crowther, Janet H., and Barry Trott. *Partnering with Purpose: A Guide to Strategic Partnership Development for Libraries and Other Organizations.* Westport, Conn.: Libraries Unlimited, 2004.

Grant Thorton, LLP. *Planned Giving: A Board Member's Perspective,* revised. Washington, D.C.: Board Source, 2003.

Greenfield, James M. *Fundraising Responsibilities of Nonprofit Boards,* second ed. Washington, D.C.: Board Source, 2009.

Herring, Mark Y. *Raising Funds with Friends Groups: A How-to-Do-It Manual for Librarians.* New York: Neal-Schuman Publishers, 2004.

Schumacher, Edward. *Capital Campaigns: Constructing a Successful Fundraising Drive.* Washington, D.C.: Board Source, 2001.

Swan, James. *Fundraising for Libraries: A How-to-Do-It Manual for Librarians.* New York: Neal-Schuman Publishers, 2002.

Worth, George. *Fearless Fundraising for Nonprofit Boards,* revised ed. Washington, D.C.: Board Source, 2003.

Chapter 12

ADVOCACY

Get your crystal ball out of storage and dust it off. Which vision of the future do you see for your library?

The Bright Future

• The library facility looks ample, well lit, and attractive. No signs of aging or wear are apparent.
• A number of staff members are in evidence, and they look relaxed and focused.
• A random scan in the stacks turns up many titles published in the last 5 years, with few older than 20 years; items are neatly and properly arranged.
• Plenty of computer workstations are visible in the patron area; most, but not all, are occupied.
• The line at checkout is short and moves quickly; several checkout stations are staffed, and the entire circulation operation seems to be humming with efficiency.

The Bleak Future

• The library facility is cramped and drab; obviously, no updating or renovation has been undertaken for a long time.
• The one staff member on the scene looks harried and overwhelmed.
• A random scan in the stacks reveals many distressed books with worn bindings and few books published in the last 5 years. Also, many items appear to be misshelved.
• The two computers available for patrons look outdated, and one appears to be out of order; at the other is a long line of irritated patrons.
• Patrons lined up at the checkout desk are subject to a heated exchange between a library staff member and a patron who claims that a recently returned book was not checked-in properly.

As a library trustee, you have a special opportunity to help usher in a bright future for your library. Conversely, if you and your fellow trustees coast along, doing as little as possible, your negligence, if not checked, could bring about a bleaker future.

Trustees and Advocacy

You and your fellow trustees have an important, special role to play: that of being an advocate for the library within the community and, especially, in interactions with government officials, business leaders, and other decision-makers. In general, we refer to this aspect of trustee responsibilities as *advocacy*.

You and the individuals with whom you share trustee responsibilities are in a unique position to advocate for the library. Because you are not paid employees of the library, you have no vested interests in any particular policies. Moreover, as library users yourselves, you view library services pretty much from the viewpoint of patrons—as opposed to the point of view of library professionals, for example. You are also taxpayers and voters in the local political entity (or in any one of the constituent political entities) and thus stakeholders in the public library.

One aspect of advocacy is public relations, which embraces all the ways the library administration publicizes its services in the community. The topic of public relations is considered in Chapter 13, which follows.

The focus in this chapter is advocacy among government officials who directly affect the library by their decision-making capabilities: municipal officials, state legislators, and state constitutional officers, as well as members of the U.S. Congress and other federal officials.

Identify Decision-Makers

The first step of effective advocacy is identifying the people in a position to affect the fate of the library's plans for providing service to the community. Local officials most directly hold the purse strings for public libraries, since libraries' primary funding comes from local property taxes. State officials may also have a major impact on Illinois libraries. They fund and oversee the Illinois State Library and allocate money for state library grants.

Federal lawmakers and officials make an impact on our Illinois libraries, too. As you have seen in Chapter 10, "Budgeting and Financial Management," the U.S. Congress funds grants to libraries through the LSTA program. Federal e-rate funding helps public libraries in Illinois pay for technologies such as Internet connections and phones, as outlined in Chapter 6, "Intellectual Freedom."

While advocacy issues frequently center on money or power, it is important to remember that library advocates must also articulately advocate for our basic principles, such as access to information and intellectual freedom. The following chart lists government officials at various levels of government who may be decision-makers for public libraries.

> Local: Mayor(s), city council members, township supervisors, county commissioners
> State: Legislative representatives, including local members of the Illinois House and Senate; the governor; the secretary of state
> Federal: U.S. representative of the congressional district in which the library resides and the state's two U.S. senators; the President

You and the other trustees, collectively, can obtain an up-to-date roster of local, state, and federal officials of concern to your library. The ILA website (www.ila.org) includes contact information such as mailing address, office phone and fax numbers, and e-mail addresses.

Advocacy Among Governmental Officials

A library board of trustees can make an important investment in the library's future by cultivating close, cordial working relationships with key government officials. This advocacy work requires time, commitment, careful coordination among board members, continual effort, and at least a little finesse. The board will probably want to designate specific trustees to stay in touch with specific officials. Following are some guidelines for the board and its representatives.

Cultivating Relationships with Government Officials . . .

- Stay current: know who the key players are and how to contact them.
- Identify officials' key staff members and cultivate relationships with them.
- Add officials to the library and Friends of the Library mailing lists.
- Make personal contacts with officials by phone or personal letter.
- Invite officials to library functions, especially those that highlight or showcase programs and services.
- Become familiar with the political process; learn about
  - the functioning of the town or city council or the county board of commissioners.
  - the legislative process at the state level.
- Know the timing of an issue, such as when the Illinois General Assembly is in session, or a local official or body is likely to act.
- Reinforce relationships by attending advocacy days in Springfield and Washington, D.C., and personally lobbying officials.

When a Particular Political Issue Looms Large

Suppose the time comes when the library board identifies a pending proposal for legislative action that could have a significant impact on the local library and public libraries in the state or region. The board may opt to swing into political action; if the trustees have worked carefully to develop a network of relationships with key government officials, the board will already have "a leg up" in its lobbying campaign.

Lobbying for a Particular Proposal . . .

- Contact the local state representative and state senator. If feasible, request a personal appointment for the board's designated representative.
- At the beginning of the appointment or phone conversation, identify yourself, your library, and the community in which you live.
- Identify the issue with which the library board is concerned; provide the following information:
  - official number of the bill in question
  - a very brief description of the bill
  - why the library board supports or opposes the measure
  - a very brief analysis of what the effects of the bill's passage or rejection might be on the library and other local public libraries
- Sum up the library board's position, listen attentively to the official's response, and then respectfully request his or her support.
- Submit a one-page summary—for example, a bullet list—of your presentation in writing. If the contact is a phone conversation, include the summary as an attachment to your follow-up thank-you letter.
- Follow up the visit or phone conversation with a personal thank-you letter, regardless of outcome.

There are definite "do's" and "don'ts" of governmental advocacy. Avoid these actions and behaviors:

Advocacy No-No's . . .

- Wasting an official's time by showing up late for an appointment
- Communicating by form letters or any other "canned" format
- Deluging officials with programmed e-mails, phone calls, letters, or other communications (A spontaneous outpouring from the public, on the other hand, is a hallowed democratic tradition, and often proves quite effective.)
- Being wordy and unfocused
- Making negative generalizations or insinuations about politicians
- Attempting to disguise costs of proposed legislation
- Characterizing the official's record or previous votes in a negative way
- Demanding, rather than requesting, the official's support
- Threatening to mobilize opposition at the next election
- Failing to send a written letter of thanks in response to a favorable gesture, such as making time available for a meeting

No matter the outcome on a particular issue, seek always to maintain cordial relations with key governmental officials.

Ways to Stay "In the Loop"

In addition to establishing contact and cultivating relationships with key government officials, you can make use of opportunities for advocacy that are provided by library organizations and associations.

Legislative Days

The American Library Association (ALA) annually sponsors "legislative days" in Washington, D.C., to provide a forum for library advocates to meet with various lawmakers. The event includes oral briefings and written materials. Visit the ALA website, http://www.ala.org/nlld, for more information.

Calls for Action

The ALA and the ILA occasionally call on members to contact their legislators about a given issue. The library board of trustees should consider making a concerted response to each such call for action.

Resources

The ILA, through its Public Policy Committee, issues pertinent information via direct e-mail announcements to ILA members. Another advocacy resource is available on the ILA website: go online to **http://www.ila.org** and select **Advocacy.**

The ALA continually monitors legislative action in the U.S. Congress. To keep current, consult the "Advocacy & Issues" page of the ALA website: http://www.ala.org/advocacy. The ALA Washington Office is a particularly useful source of federal legislative information relevant to libraries.

Specific Titles

Comito, Lauren, Aligae Geraci, and Christian Zabriskie. *Grassroots Library Advocacy.* Chicago: American Library Association, 2012.

Crowther, Janet H., and Barry Trott. *Partnering with Purpose: A Guide to Strategic Partnership Development for Libraries and Other Organizations.* Westport, Conn.: Libraries Unlimited, 2004.

Halsey, Richard S. *Lobbying for Public and School Libraries: A History and Political Playbook.* Lanham, Md.: Scarecrow Press, 2003.

Kush, Christopher. *Grassroot Games: Preparing Your Advocates for the Political Arena.* Washington, D.C.: American Society of Association Executives, 2002.

Reed, Sally Gardner. *Making the Case for Your Library: A How-to-Do-It Manual.* New York: Neal-Schuman Publishers, 2001.

Legislative Terms

In order to be an effective advocate, you need to know the language of government. The following is a list of basic terms used to describe the people, places, and processes of government. Review these terms to better understand the legislative process, and use these terms to better communicate with your public officials.

Act: A bill that has been made law by passing both houses of the legislature, and that has been signed by the governor, filed without the governor's signature, or passed by both houses of the legislature over the governor's veto.

Administrative Rule: Any agency directive, standard, regulation, or statement of general applicability that implements, interprets, or prescribes law or policy, or describes the procedure or practice requirements of any agency.

Amendment: Any alteration made, or proposed to be made, in a bill or motion by adding, changing, substituting, or omitting.

Appropriation: A law which details how the government's money will be spent.

Back Door Referendum: A limitation on the power of government to take certain actions that a political subdivision has already initiated. The Illinois Compiled Statutes (10 ILCS 5/28-2) define this as the submission of a public question to the voters of a political subdivision, initiated by a petition of the voters, to determine whether an action by the government shall be adopted or rejected. If a majority of the voters oppose the action in the referendum, the government is precluded from taking that action. The law specifies which actions may be subject to back door referendums.

Bicameral: A legislature consisting of two houses, typically the senate and the house of representatives.

Bill: A measure that creates new law, amends or repeals existing law, appropriates money, prescribes fees, transfers functions from one agency to another, provides penalties, or takes other action. The proposed law is introduced during a session for consideration by the legislature, and is identified numerically in order of its presentation.

Budget: Legislation which details both the receipt and allocation of state funds. The governor annually presents a proposed budget for consideration by the legislature. The legislature may accept or alter any portion of the governor's proposed budget, and must pass the budget as one or more individual bills. The governor may then accept the budget as passed by the legislature, or make changes to all or some of the individual line items contained in the budget. Finally, the legislature may accept any changes by the governor on a simple majority vote, or restore funding to the levels originally passed by overriding the governor's changes on a supermajority vote.

Calendar: A listing of the bills (and other proposed legislative matters) pending in the chamber. The calendar also lists meetings of committees scheduled for that day or for the next several days. Calendars are available to the public each day the legislature is in regular session.

Capitol: The state house, or capitol building. Its address is: 207 State House, Springfield, IL 62706.

Caucus: "Caucus" is used as both a noun and a verb. A caucus, *n.*, is a group of people who share something in common (e.g. they are members of the same political party, such as the "Senate Republican Caucus" or the "House Democratic Caucus," or come from the same area of the state, such as the "Downstate Caucus," or share something else in common, such as the "Sportsman Caucus"). When these people caucus, *v.*, they meet to discuss policy questions, to select caucus leaders, and to take positions as a group on legislative proposals.

Chairman: The legislator appointed by the chamber's presiding officer to serve as the presiding officer of a particular committee.

Chamber: The room where legislators gather as a body to formally conduct state business; the House or Senate floor. It may also be used to refer collectively to all legislators in a particular house of the legislature.

Commissions: Often composed of both legislators and public members, they are primarily created to study and propose legislation on specific and usually more complex issues. Commissions can be either temporary or permanent.

Committee of the Whole: The entire membership of the house or senate, which may be convened to hear testimony on bills of particular importance.

Companion Bill: One of two identical bills introduced in both houses.

Conference Committee: A committee set up for the sole purpose of reconciling disagreements between the House and Senate on amendments to a bill. Conference committees do not typically meet as a group, but rather a majority of the members are required to sign any agreement which then may be presented for a final vote in each chamber.

Conflict of Interest: Any interest, financial or otherwise, any business or professional activity, or any obligation which is incompatible with the proper discharge of a person's public duties.

Constitutional Officers: Officials who serve state-wide in positions created by the Illinois constitution including the governor, lieutenant governor, attorney general, secretary of state, comptroller, treasurer, and auditor general. All except the auditor general are elected positions.

Constituent: A person residing within an elected official's district or area of representation.

Convene: To assemble or call together.

Cosponsor. Two or more legislators proposing a bill or resolution.

District: That division of the state represented by a legislator which is distinguished numerically and determined on the basis of population. The area of a district is supposed to be geographically both compact and contiguous.

Executive Branch: The branch of state government led by the governor and comprised of state departments, agencies, boards and commissions which are responsible for the execution, implementation and enforcement of state laws.

First Reading: The recitation on the chamber floor of a bill or resolution's number, title, and brief description as read by the clerk of the chamber upon introduction in either house. After the first reading, the measure is referred to the chamber's rules committee by the chamber's presiding officer. The bill or resolution may then be referred to a relevant substantive committee. The Illinois Constitution requires that every bill must be read three times on three separate legislative session days in each chamber in order to pass.

Fiscal Note: Statement as to the estimated cost of legislation having a fiscal impact. The fiscal impact note is prepared and filed with the clerk of the chamber by the appropriate state agency or department. If a fiscal note has been requested by a legislator, the legislation cannot be considered until the fiscal note has been properly filed.

Floor: A colloquialism describing the interior of either chamber, sometimes distinguishing the membership from the presiding officer; matters before the full chamber may be referred to as "on the floor."

Gallery: Areas of both chambers where public visitors may observe the legislature in session.

HB: House Bill.

Hearing: A public meeting of a legislative committee held for the purpose of taking testimony concerning proposed legislation. Typically following testimony and an opportunity for questions, committee members will vote on the matter.

House of Representatives (Illinois): The legislative body of 118 members, called representatives, each of whom represents a district of approximately 109,000 Illinois citizens.

Joint Session: Joint sessions are meetings of the House and Senate together that are primarily ceremonial; for example, to hear the governor's state of the state and budget addresses, or to hear a distinguished guest. Bills are never passed in a joint session.

Journal: The printed daily proceedings of each chamber.

Judicial Branch: The branch of State government made up of the Illinois Supreme Court, five districts of the appellate courts with fifty-three judges, and twenty-three judicial circuits that have more than 852 circuit and associate judges. The Illinois Supreme Court interprets the Illinois Constitution and laws, and hears final arguments in certain civil and criminal cases.

Leadership: The presiding elected officers of each house; the president of the Senate and the speaker of the House. They are elected by a majority of the members of their respective chambers when the body organizes for a legislative session following a general election. "Leadership" also refers to the minority leaders in each chamber, who are elected by a majority vote of their respective caucuses. On occasion, "leadership" is also meant to refer to assistant majority and minority leaders who are appointed by the presiding officers and minority leaders.

Legislative Branch: The branch of state government comprised of the Illinois General Assembly and various support agencies responsible for the passage of laws.

Legislative Liaison: A person designated by a state agency to act as its "lobbyist." The liaisons are not registered as lobbyists and on occasion have access to the floors of both chambers.

Legislative Reference Bureau: The Legislative Reference Bureau, often simply referred to as "LRB," is comprised of attorneys paid by the state who assist legislators in drafting proposed bills and resolutions. Between sessions, this bill-drafting agency studies Illinois statutes for inconsistencies and mistakes, and suggests ways to simplify statutes.

Line Item Veto: The governor may veto an item in an appropriation bill without vetoing the entire bill, and may also increase or decrease a particular appropriation. These actions are subject to acceptance or override by the legislature.

Local Government: Under the Illinois Constitution, local governments include general purpose units such as counties (102 in the state), townships (85 counties have them), and municipalities (1,295), and special purpose units including school, park, fire, library, and sewage special districts. There are a total of 7,067 units of local government in Illinois.

Lobbyist: A person who is employed by an individual, organization, association or business to represent its interests before the legislature. The term derives from the fact that lobbyists usually frequent the areas (lobbies) adjacent to the chambers of the senate and the house, either seeking to buttonhole legislators as they walk to and from the chambers or await legislative action which might affect their clients' interests. Individual citizens may also "lobby" their legislators on matters of concern to them. Illinois law requires persons (excluding public employees, officials and staff) who seek to encourage the passage, defeat, or modification of legislation to register as lobbyists.

Majority Leader: A legislator selected by the speaker of the House. Sometimes this person is responsible for the development and implementation of the caucus agenda, the debate on bills which the party supports or documentation, decisions on floor tactics, and assisting in the selection of committee members of the party.

Minority Leader: A legislator elected by his or her peers to lead the party in the minority in his or her house and having similar duties as the majority leader.

Minority Spokesperson: Designated by the minority leader, this person serves as the chief spokesperson for the minority members of a standing committee.

Motion: A formal procedural proposal offered by a legislator requesting that the body take a particular action.

Passage: Favorable action on a measure before either house.

Penalty Clauses: Sections of bills which lay out criminal or civil penalties for violation of the law.

Per diem: Literally meaning "For the day." It is a set payment to legislators for travel, food and lodging expenses when the Legislature is in regular session.

Perfunctory Session: An abbreviated but official meeting of either chamber in order to conduct procedural business and other "Housekeeping chores." An example would be introduction of bills and filing of motions. No roll call votes are permitted in perfunctory sessions and typically legislators do not come to the Capitol in Springfield.

Point of Inquiry: A request from a legislator on the floor, or from a committee member in committee, asking a question regarding the status of a legislative matter or applicable rule. Typically, such questions are about issues such as parliamentary procedure.

Point of Order: A request from a legislator on the floor, or from a committee member in committee, requesting a ruling from the presiding officer regarding the application of the rules or calling attention to a breach of order or the rules.

Point of Personal Privilege: A way in which a legislator can get the immediate attention of the presiding officer on the floor of either chamber. It is typically used to introduce guests or recognize a particular person or issue.

Postponed Consideration: Legislation that has not received the required number of votes for passage may, at the request of the sponsor, be placed on the order of "postponed consideration," where it can be given a second opportunity for passage at a later time. In order to be placed on postponed consideration the matter must have received a minimum number of votes as established by rule.

President of the Senate: The presiding officer of the Senate, elected by a majority of the members of the Senate when that body organizes at the beginning of its two year general assembly term.

Presiding Officer: Specifically meaning the speaker of the House and president of the Senate, but also meaning any legislator asked by the speaker or president to preside over a particular session or committee.

Primary Election: A preliminary election in which only registered voters who self-identify as belonging to an established political party vote to nominate that party's candidates for office.

Quorum: The minimum number of members required to be present before business can be transacted. The presence of a majority of the elected members in the chamber constitutes a quorum; 60 members in the Illinois House and 30 members in the Illinois Senate.

Reapportionment: Periodic redrawing of the geographic areas within the state into districts for election purposes from which legislators are elected.

Recess: Recess is the period of time when the Illinois General Assembly or either of its houses is not in session after once being convened. Recesses include stated periods, such as those for lunch, and informal periods, when the members await the presiding officer's call to return. An informal recess may be necessitated by a caucus, or while the House awaits the arrival of the Senate for a joint session.

Reconsideration: Motion which, when approved, gives rise to another vote annulling or reaffirming an action previously taken.

Referendum: The submission of a proposed public measure or law to the vote of the people for ratification or rejection. The manner in which this is done by library boards is prescribed by Illinois law.

Regular Session: A session day in which legislators are expected to be at the Capitol for the conduct of legislative business. Contrasted with a perfunctory session day.

Roll Calls: A roll call electronically records "for the record" each individual legislator's vote on third readings, as well as on contested amendments or motions. A "verified" roll call is when each legislator is specifically called by name and asked to orally confirm their vote as recorded.

Rules: Rules are procedures adopted by each chamber governing its organization, conduct, order of business, bill procedure, and so forth.

Rules Committee: Comprised of legislators in leadership from both parties but controlled by the majority party. Its most powerful function is to assign, or refuse to assign, bills and resolutions to substantive committees for a hearing or for consideration on the floor.

SB: Senate Bill.

Second Reading: Like First Reading, a recitation of the bill or resolution's number, title, and brief description by the clerk of the chamber. Second Reading occurs after the measure has been referred to committee, worked on, and reported back to the floor for a vote. It is also the stage at which bills may be amended on the floor. The Illinois Constitution requires that every bill must be read three times on three separate legislative session days in each chamber in order to pass.

Senate (Illinois): The legislative body consisting of fifty-nine members, called senators, each representing districts of approximately 218,000 Illinois citizens.

Session: The period of time in which the Illinois General Assembly officially convenes. The regular session begins in January and typically ends around June 1st. The Veto session is typically six days in November. Special sessions may be convened at the call of the governor or the legislative leaders.

Shell Bill: A bill with no substantive language, but used as a "placeholder," if needed, to introduce new legislative initiatives at a later date.

Sine Die: Final adjournment. No date is set for reconvening. A two year general assembly term ends when the Legislature adjourns sine die.

Speaker of the House: The presiding officer of the Illinois House of Representatives, elected by a majority of the members of the house when the house organizes at the beginning of its two year general assembly term.

Special Session: Called by either the governor or the joint leadership of both houses. Special sessions address specific issues such as emergency budget matters.

Sponsor: The legislator(s) who introduces a measure. The name of this person is printed at the top of the measure. In very rare occasions, a committee may also act as sponsor of a legislative measure.

Statute: A codified law. "Codify" means "to arrange laws systematically." A codified law is one that has been incorporated into that section of the Illinois Compiled Statutes that it amends, modifies, or accompanies.

Sunset: The provision of a legislative matter which calls for the automatic repeal of the measure at a certain date or upon the happening of some event.

Sunshine Laws: Meant to refer to a variety of laws which call for openness in government including the Illinois Open Meetings Act and the Freedom of Information Act, but also many other acts which detail how public business is to be conducted.

Table: To table is a procedural motion to prevent a bill, resolution or other motion from being considered. There are also methods for a tabled bill to be reactivated.

Third Reading: As in First or Second Readings, a recitation of a measure's number, title, and brief description by the clerk of the chamber on the floor before final consideration by either house. The Illinois Constitution requires that every bill must be read three times on three separate legislative session days in each chamber in order to pass.

Veto: Action by the governor in disapproval of a measure. On substantive (non-appropriation) bills, the governor may "total veto" a bill, which means that he/she disapproves of it in its entirety, or "amendatorily veto" a bill, which means that he/she would accept the legislation if the amendatory changes were made. The legislature can override a total veto or amendatory veto by a three-fifths supermajority vote, or may accept the changes of an amendatory veto by a simple majority vote. On appropriation bills, the governor may totally veto the bill, or make line item changes to delete a particular line item appropriation, or increase or decrease a line item. Again the legislature may override the governor's veto of any line item appropriation by a supermajority vote, or accept the veto by a simple majority.

Chapter 13

PUBLIC RELATIONS

Public relations (PR) embraces all the ways a library publicizes its programs and services in the community. The main goal of public relations is to raise people's awareness about the role (or potential role) of the library in their lives and in the community. A good public relations program will mobilize support among civic organizations, business leaders, taxpayers and voters generally.

A Formal Public Relations Policy

Expressing sincere intent to foster good public relations isn't enough; the library board of trustees needs to plan, budget, and implement a carefully thought-out PR policy on an annual basis. To make an effective plan, the board needs to maintain various contacts in the community and look for good PR opportunities, as well as work closely with library staff who plan and present regular library programming.

Based on a number of inputs, especially including events suggested by community contacts, the board must budget adequate funds. Part of the budget might detail specific events and campaigns, but a significant portion of funds should be reserved for "ad-hoc" PR activities of which the board may not be aware until later in the fiscal year.

To target successful PR outreach, the board should develop contacts widely in the community, as suggested in the following list.

Cultivate Contacts among Groups in the Community . . .

- Business groups, such as the Chamber of Commerce, and individual business leaders. There is nothing wrong with focusing public relations or fundraising efforts on larger companies in the library service area. They may be in a position to contribute generously to the library and may have a large captive audience in their employee base.
- Associations for ethnic groups with strong representation in the library service area
- Civic organizations, such as the League of Women Voters
- Service organizations, such as the Rotary Club
- Literacy advocacy groups
- Churches, synagogues, and mosques
- Professionals in the news media

- Administrators and faculty of schools
- School PTA's
- Youth service organizations, such as Boy Scouts and Girl Scouts
- Book clubs
- Senior citizen centers

Media

Obviously, there are many ways to communicate with the public. Most have associated costs. A good public relations program should use a wide variety of media, but choices may be limited somewhat by budget constraints.

The costs of having trustees or staff make presentations to local civic or other groups are minimal, and a good public relations program will make use of these opportunities to the fullest extent.

A few communications media that may be useful in a PR campaign are suggested here.

Types of Media To Use in PR Campaigns . . .

- Bookmarks—"freebies" to give out in the library and in local bookstores
- Brochures
- Posters
- Displays and exhibits in public places
- Photographs
- Local newspapers, magazines
- Dedicated website for the library
- Radio
- Social media (Facebook, Twitter, etc.)
- Television (network or cable)
- Website

Making Public Presentations

Suppose you are the designated representative to make a presentation on behalf of the public library to a local civic group. A few helpful tips follow.

Tips for Effective Presentations . . .

- At the start, acknowledge the group and express appreciation for the invitation to speak.
- Explain your role as a trustee of the library.
- Make use of graphics; for example, a short slide show highlighting library facilities, holdings, programs, and staff would be a good audience warm-up.
- Incorporate anecdotes and stories to enliven content.
- Present the library in a positive light; highlight plans for expansion of services and programs or improvements in facilities.
- Illustrate ways in which the library is making good use of the public funding on which it depends.
- Highlight the library's technological services, if appropriate.
- Emphasize the commitment of public libraries to freedom of information and equality of access to information.
- Give audience members an opportunity to ask questions; answer as honestly as possible.
- Distribute copies of the library's latest newsletter or a brochure that summarizes the library's programs and services.
- Be sure to cite the URL (universal resource locator—the online address) of the library website, if one exists.

- Always maintain a cordial, friendly demeanor.

Learning from the Public

In contacts and communications with various sectors of the public, library administrators hope to receive glowing reports about community members' library experiences. If the response is otherwise—for example, facilities or services are perceived as inadequate, staff as unfriendly and unresponsive, the collection as poorly maintained—then you and the other trustees and library staff should seize the opportunity to put things right.

Public dissatisfaction might cloak ultimate support for expanded funding for library programs and services. The board of trustees might reorient the library's public relations program to convincing community members that their concerns can be addressed by an expanded program and to developing a fundraising campaign.

If staff relations with the community appear to be a problem, discuss this issue with the library director. It may be advisable to launch a staff training program. To plan and carry out such a program, seek assistance from the state library, and associations such as the ILA and ALA.

Friends of the Library

United for Libraries: the Association of Library Trustees, Advocates, Friends and Foundations is a national membership organization especially for people just like you. The organization provides resources and information through its website, annual meetings and conferences, and other programs. For more information, go online to the group's website at http://www.ala.org/altaff.

Help from Associations

The ALA and ILA occasionally sponsor campaigns to showcase services of public libraries. Visit the websites of these organizations to check for such resources.

For example, ALA sponsors the Campaign for America's Libraries, known as "@ your library," an ongoing public education campaign to communicate the value of public libraries and librarians to the public. To find out more, go to www.atyourlibrary.org.

Resources

Buschman, John E. *Dismantling the Public Sphere: Situating and Sustaining Librarianship in the Age of the New Public Philosophy.* Westport, Conn.: Libraries Unlimited, 2003.

Dowd, Nancy, Mary Evangeliste, and Jonathan Silberman. *Bite-sized Marketing: Realistic Solutions for the Overworked Librarian.* Chicago: American Library Association, 2010.

Gould, Mark R. *The Library PR Handbook: High Impact Communications.* Chicago: American Library Association, 2009.

Jones, Patrick. *Running a Successful Library Card Campaign: A How-to-Do-It Manual,* second ed. New York: Neal-Schuman Publishers, 2002.

Matthews, Joseph R. *Measuring for Results: The Dimensions of Public Library Effectiveness.* Westport, Conn.: Libraries Unlimited, 2003.

Smallwood, Carol. *Librarians as Community Partners: An Outreach Handbook.* Chicago: American Library Association, 2010.

Walters, Suzanne. *Library Marketing That Works!* New York: Neal-Schuman Publishers, 2004.

Wolfe, Lisa A. *Library Public Relations, Promotions, and Communications: A How-to-Do-It Manual,* second ed. New York: Neal-Schuman Publishers, 2003.

Chapter 14

TRUSTEE CONTINUING EDUCATION

If you have read the preceding chapters in this book, you are well aware of the need to hone knowledge and skills in a number of diverse areas to function effectively as a library trustee. During your tenure on the board, you will likely be confronted by changes in the community, technological innovations, and shifting political and cultural currents; keeping yourself up-to-date will pose a considerable challenge. To answer this challenge, you should plan to take advantage of opportunities for continuing education.

Here are a few basic ideas for trustee continuing education.

- Use the chapters of this book to conduct trustee education "classes" on a regular basis.
- Ask the library director to conduct seminars for trustees (and others, as appropriate) on topics such as Intellectual Freedom, Patron Privacy, Collection Maintenance, Library Resources, or Internet Use Policy.
- Visit other libraries in the library system or state and request meetings with the library director and trustees of those libraries; attend board meetings of other libraries.
- Ask an attorney to give a presentation on legal issues related to libraries and library trusteeship.
- Join the American Library Association (ALA) and the Illinois Library Association (ILA). The costs for these memberships are appropriate to pay from the library's budget.
- Attend one or more library workshops or conferences annually.

Budget

Don't overlook trustee continuing education when developing the annual budget. Include funds for trustee memberships in associations, attendance at workshops and conferences, book purchases, and other relevant expenses.

Develop guidelines for trustee and staff continuing education expenses so participants are clear about what expenses will be reimbursed and what documentation is required for accounting purposes.

The remainder of this chapter is a list of resources that may be useful in planning trustee continuing education.

Resources

Various topics offered at the Illinois State Library Administrative Ready Reference web page
Go online to http://www.webjunction.org/partners/Illinois/il-topics/readyref.html

Illinois Library Laws & Rules, 2012. Available for purchase, http://www.ila.

Serving Our Public 2.0: Standards for Illinois Public Libraries, Available for purchase: http://
www.ila.org

United for Libraries: the Association for Library Trustees, Advocates, Friends and
Foundations, an excellent resource for conferences and workshops
Go online to http://www.ala.org/ala/alta/altaff

Wright, George B. *Beyond Nominating: A Guide to Gaining and Sustaining Successful Not-For-
Profit-Boards.* Portland, Ore.: C3 Publications, 1996.

Appendix G, "Selected Resources"

For **Advocacy** topics, see the Resources section at the end of Chapter 12, "Advocacy."

Appendices

Appendix A

Library Bill of Rights

The American Library Association affirms that all libraries are forums for information and ideas, and that the following basic policies should guide their services.

1. Books and other library resources should be provided for the interest, information, and enlightenment of all people of the community the library serves. Materials should not be excluded because of the origin, background, or views of those contributing to their creation.
2. Libraries should provide materials and information presenting all points of view on current and historical issues. Materials should not be proscribed or removed because of partisan or doctrinal disapproval.
3. Libraries should challenge censorship in the fulfillment of their responsibility to provide information and enlightenment.
4. Libraries should cooperate with all persons and groups concerned with resisting abridgment of free expression and free access to ideas.
5. A person's right to use a library should not be denied or abridged because of origin, age, background, or views.
6. Libraries which make exhibit spaces and meeting rooms available to the public they serve should make such facilities available on an equitable basis, regardless of the beliefs or affiliations of individuals or groups requesting their use.

Adopted June 19, 1939 by the ALA Council; amended October 14, 1944; June 18, 1948. Amended February 2, 1961, June 27, 1967, and January 23, 1980; inclusion of "age" reaffirmed January 23, 1996, by the ALA Council. Reprinted with permission from the American Library Association.

Interpretations to the Library Bill of Rights *and policy guidance regarding intellectual freedom concerns*

Over the years, questions have arisen concerning the application of the *Library Bill of Rights* principles to specific library practices. For example, a 1951 Peoria, Illinois, case involving films in the public library required the association to clarify the application of the *Library Bill of Rights* to nonprint materials. A recommendation by the Intellectual Freedom and the Audio-Visual Board resulted in the ALA Council's adding an interpretive footnote explaining that the *Library Bill of Rights* applies to all materials and media of communication used or collected by libraries.

To date, the following interpretations have been adopted by the ALA Council and are available at the ALA website, www.ala.org/oif:

- Access for Children and Young People to Videotapes and Other Nonprint Formats
- Access to Digital Information, Services, and Networks
- Access to Library Resources and Services regardless of Gender Identity, Gender Expression, or Sexual Orientation
- Access to Resources in the School Library Media Program
- Challenged Materials
- Diversity in Collection Development
- Economic Barriers to Information Access
- Evaluating Library Collections
- Exhibit Spaces and Bulletin Boards
- Expurgation of Library Materials
- Free Access to Libraries for Minors
- Importance of Education on Intellectual Freedom
- Intellectual Freedom Principles for Academic Libraries
- Labeling and Rating Systems
- Library-Initiated Programs as a Resource
- Minors and Internet Interactivity
- Meeting Rooms
- Privacy
- Restricted Access to Library Materials
- Services to People with Disabilities
- The Universal Right to Free Expression

In addition, the ALA provides the following policy guidance regarding intellectual freedom concerns:

- Dealing with Concerns about Library Resources
- Developing a Confidentiality Policy
- Guidelines and Consideration for Internet Use Policy
- Guidelines for the Development of Policies and Procedures regarding User Behavior and Library Usage
- Guidelines for the Development and Implementation of Policies, Regulations and Procedures Affecting Access to Library Materials, Services and Facilities
- Policy on Confidentiality of Library Records
- Policy concerning the Confidentiality of Personally Identifiable Information about Library Users
- Policy on Government Intimidation

Appendix B

The Freedom to Read

The freedom to read is essential to our democracy. It is continuously under attack. Private groups and public authorities in various parts of the country are working to remove books from sale, to censor textbooks, to label "controversial" books, to distribute lists of "objectionable" books or authors, and to purge libraries. These actions apparently rise from a view that our national tradition of free expression is no longer valid; that censorship and suppression are needed to avoid the subversion of politics and the corruption of morals. We, as citizens devoted to the use of books and as librarians and publishers responsible for disseminating them, wish to assert the public interest in the preservation of the freedom to read.

We are deeply concerned about these attempts at suppression. Most such attempts rest on a denial of the fundamental premise of democracy: that the ordinary citizen, by exercising critical judgment, will accept the good and reject the bad. The censors, public and private, assume that they should determine what is good and what is bad for their fellow-citizens.

We trust Americans to recognize propaganda, and to reject it. We do not believe they need the help of censors to assist them in this task. We do not believe they are prepared to sacrifice their heritage of a free press in order to be "protected" against what others think may be bad for them. We believe they still favor free enterprise in ideas and expression

We are aware, of course, that books are not alone in being subjected to efforts at suppression. We are aware that these efforts are related to a larger pattern of pressures being brought against education, the press, films, radio and television. The problem is not only one of actual censorship. The shadow of fear cast by these pressures leads, we suspect, to an even larger voluntary curtailment of expression by those who seek to avoid controversy.

Such pressure toward conformity is perhaps natural to a time of uneasy change and pervading fear. Especially when so many of our apprehensions are directed against an ideology, the expression of a dissident idea becomes a thing feared in itself, and we tend to move against it as against a hostile deed, with suppression.

And yet suppression is never more dangerous than in such a time of social tension. Freedom has given the United States the elasticity to endure strain. Freedom keeps open the path of novel and creative solutions, and enables change to come by choice. Every silencing of a heresy, every enforcement of an orthodoxy, diminishes the toughness and resilience of our society and leaves it the less able to deal with stress.

Now as always in our history, books are among our greatest instruments of freedom. They are almost the only means for making generally available ideas or manners of expression that can initially command only a small audience. They are the natural medium for the new idea and the untried voice from which come the original contributions to social growth. They are essential to the extended discussion which serious thought requires, and to the accumulation of knowledge and ideas into organized collections.

We believe that free communication is essential to the preservation of a free society and a creative culture. We believe that these pressures towards conformity present the danger of limiting the range and variety of inquiry and expression on which our democracy and our culture depend. We believe that every American community must jealously guard the freedom to publish and to circulate, in order to preserve its own freedom to read. We believe that publishers and librarians have a profound responsibility to give validity to that freedom to read by making it possible for the readers to choose freely from a variety of offerings.

The freedom to read is guaranteed by the Constitution. Those with faith in free people will stand firm on these constitutional guarantees of essential rights and will exercise the responsibilities that accompany these rights. We therefore affirm these propositions:

1. It is in the public interest for publishers and librarians to make available the widest diversity of views and expressions, including those which are unorthodox or unpopular with the majority.

   Creative thought is by definition new, and what is new is different. The bearer of every new thought is a rebel until that idea is refined and tested. Totalitarian systems attempt to maintain themselves in power by the ruthless suppression of any concept which challenges the established orthodoxy. The power of a democratic system to adapt to change is vastly strengthened by the freedom of its citizens to choose widely from among conflicting opinions offered freely to them.

   To stifle every nonconformist idea at birth would mark the end of the democratic process. Furthermore, only through the constant activity of weighing and selecting can the democratic mind attain the strength demanded by times like these. We need to know not only what we believe but why we believe it.

2. Publishers, librarians and booksellers do not need to endorse every idea or presentation contained in the books they make available. It would conflict with the public interest for them to establish their own political, moral or aesthetic views as a standard for determining what books should be published or circulated.

   Publishers and librarians serve the educational process by helping to make available knowledge and ideas required for the growth of the mind and the increase of learning. They do not foster education by imposing as mentors the patterns of their own thought. The people should have the freedom to read and consider a broader range of ideas than those that may be held by any single librarian or publisher or government or church. It is wrong that what one can read should be confined to what another thinks proper.

3. It is contrary to the public interest for publishers or librarians to determine the acceptability of a book on the basis of the personal history or political affiliations of the author.

   A book should be judged as a book. No art or literature can flourish if it is to be measured by the political views or private lives of its creators. No society of free people can flourish which draws up lists of writers to whom it will not listen, whatever they may have to say.

4. There is no place in our society for efforts to coerce the taste of others, to confine adults to the reading matter deemed suitable for adolescents, or to inhibit the efforts of writers to achieve artistic expression.

   To some, much of modern literature is shocking. But is not much of life itself shocking? We cut off literature at the source if we prevent writers from dealing with the stuff of life. Parents and teachers have a responsibility to prepare the young to meet the diversity of experiences in life to which they will be exposed, as they have a responsibility to help them learn to think critically for themselves. These are affirmative responsibilities, not to be discharged simply by preventing them from reading works for which they are not yet prepared. In these matters taste differs, and taste cannot be legislated; nor can machinery be devised which will suit the demands of one group without limiting the freedom of others.

5. It is not in the public interest to force a reader to accept with any book the prejudgment of a label characterizing the book or author as subversive or dangerous.

   The ideal of labeling presupposes the existence of individuals or groups with wisdom to determine by authority what is good or bad for the citizen. It presupposes that individuals must be directed in making up their minds about the ideas they examine. But Americans do not need others to do their thinking for them.

6. It is the responsibility of publishers and librarians, as guardians of the people's freedom to read, to contest encroachments upon that freedom by individuals or groups seeking to impose their own standards or tastes upon the community at large.

   It is inevitable in the give and take of the democratic process that the political, the moral, or the aesthetic concepts of an individual or group will occasionally collide with those of another individual or group. In a free society individuals are free to determine for themselves what they wish to read, and each group is free to determine what it will recommend to its freely associated members. But no group has the right to take the law into its own hands, and to impose its own concept of politics or morality upon other members of a democratic society. Freedom is no freedom if it is accorded only to the accepted and the inoffensive.

7. It is the responsibility of publishers and librarians to give full meaning to the freedom to read by providing books that enrich the quality and diversity of thought and expression. By the exercise of this affirmative responsibility, they can demonstrate that the answer to a bad book is a good one, the answer to a bad idea is a good one.

The freedom to read is of little consequence when expended on the trivial; it is frustrated when the reader cannot obtain matter fit for that reader's purpose. What is needed is not only the absence of restraint, but the positive provision of opportunity for the people to read the best that has been thought and said. Books are the major channel by which the intellectual inheritance is handed down, and the principal means of its testing and growth. The defense of their freedom and integrity, and the enlargement of their service to society, requires of all publishers and librarians the utmost of their faculties, and deserves of all citizens the fullest of their support.

We state these propositions neither lightly nor as easy generalizations. We here stake out a lofty claim for the value of books. We do so because we believe that they are good, possessed of enormous variety and usefulness, worthy of cherishing and keeping free. We realize that the application of these propositions may mean the dissemination of ideas and manners of expression that are repugnant to many persons. We do not state these propositions in the comfortable belief that what people read is unimportant. We believe rather that what people read is deeply important; that ideas can be dangerous; but that the suppression of ideas is fatal to a democratic society. Freedom itself is a dangerous way of life, but it is ours.

This statement was originally issued in May of 1953 by the Westchester Conference of the American Library Association and the American Book Publishers Council, which in 1970 consolidated with the American Educational Publishers Institute to become the Association of American Publishers.

Adopted June 25, 1953; revised January 28, 1972, January 16, 1991, by the ALA Council and the AAP Freedom to Read Committee.

A Joint Statement by: American Library Association & Association of American Publishers.

Reprinted with permission from the American Library Association.

Appendix C

Freedom to View Statement

The freedom to view, along with the freedom to speak, to hear, and to read, is protected by the First Amendment to the Constitution of the United States. In a free society, there is no place for censorship of any medium of expression. Therefore these principles are affirmed:

1. To provide the broadest access to film, video, and other audiovisual materials because they are a means for the communication of ideas. Liberty of circulation is essential to insure the constitutional guarantees of freedom of expression.

2. To protect the confidentiality of all individuals and institutions using film, video, and other audiovisual materials.

3. To provide film, video, and other audiovisual materials which represent a diversity of views and expression. Selection of a work does not constitute or imply agreement with or approval of the content.

4. To provide a diversity of viewpoints without the constraint of labeling or prejudging film, video, or other audiovisual materials on the basis of the moral, religious, or political beliefs of the producer or filmmaker or on the basis of controversial content.

5. To contest vigorously, by all lawful means, every encroachment upon the public's freedom to view.

This statement was originally drafted by the Freedom to View Committee of the American Film and Video Association (formerly the Educational Film Library Association) and was adopted by the AFVA Board of Directors in February 1979. This statement was updated and approved by the AFVA Board of Directors in 1989.

Endorsed by the ALA Council January 10, 1990.

Reprinted with permission from the American Library Association.

Appendix D

Libraries: An American Value

Libraries in America are cornerstones of the communities they serve. Free access to the books, ideas, resources, and information in America's libraries is imperative for education, employment, enjoyment, and self-government.

Libraries are a legacy to each generation, offering the heritage of the past and the promise of the future. To ensure that libraries flourish and have the freedom to promote and protect the public good in the 21st century, we believe certain principles must be guaranteed.

To that end, we affirm this contract with the people we serve:

- We defend the constitutional rights of all individuals, including children and teenagers, to use the library's resources and services;
- We value our nation's diversity and strive to reflect that diversity by providing a full spectrum of resources and services to the communities we serve;
- We affirm the responsibility and the right of all parents and guardians to guide their own children's use of the library and its resources and services;
- We connect people and ideas by helping each person select from and effectively use the library's resources;
- We protect each individual's privacy and confidentiality in the use of library resources and services;
- We protect the rights of individuals to express their opinions about library resources and services;
- We celebrate and preserve our democratic society by making available the widest possible range of viewpoints, opinions and ideas, so that all individuals have the opportunity to become lifelong learners—informed, literate, educated, and culturally enriched.

Change is constant, but these principles transcend change and endure in a dynamic technological, social, and political environment.

By embracing these principles, libraries in the United States can contribute to a future that values and protects freedom of speech in a world that celebrates both our similarities and our differences, respects individuals and their beliefs, and holds all persons truly equal and free.

Adopted by the ALA Council, February 3, 1999.
Reprinted with permission from the American Library Association.

Appendix E

Code of Ethics

As members of the American Library Association, we recognize the importance of codifying and making known to the profession and to the general public the ethical principles that guide the work of librarians, other professionals providing information services, library trustees and library staffs.

Ethical dilemmas occur when values are in conflict. The American Library Association Code of Ethics states the values to which we are committed, and embodies the ethical responsibilities of the profession in this changing information environment.

We significantly influence or control the selection, organization, preservation, and dissemination of information. In a political system grounded in an informed citizenry, we are members of a profession explicitly committed to intellectual freedom and the freedom of access to information. We have a special obligation to ensure the free flow of information and ideas to present and future generations.

The principles of this Code are expressed in broad statements to guide ethical decision making. These statements provide a framework; they cannot and do not dictate conduct to cover particular situations.

I.   We provide the highest level of service to all library users through appropriate and usefully organized resources; equitable service policies; equitable access; and accurate, unbiased, and courteous responses to all requests.

II.   We uphold the principles of intellectual freedom and resist all efforts to censor library resources.

III. We protect each library user's right to privacy and confidentiality with respect to information sought or received and resources consulted, borrowed, acquired or transmitted.

IV.   We respect intellectual property rights and advocate balance between the interests of information users and rights holders.

V.   We treat co-workers and other colleagues with respect, fairness and good faith, and advocate conditions of employment that safeguard the rights and welfare of all employees of our institutions.

VI.   We do not advance private interests at the expense of library users, colleagues, or our employing institutions.

VII. We distinguish between our personal convictions and professional duties and do not allow our personal beliefs to interfere with fair representation of the aims of our institutions or the provision of access to their information resources.

VIII. We strive for excellence in the profession by maintaining and enhancing our own knowledge and skills, by encouraging the professional development of co-workers, and by fostering the aspirations of potential members of the profession.

Adopted at the 1939 Midwinter Meeting by the ALA Council; amended June 30, 1981; June 28, 1995; and January 22, 2008.

Reprinted with permission from the American Library Association.

Appendix F

Ethics Statement for Public Library Trustees

- Trustees in the capacity of trust upon them, shall observe ethical standards with absolute truth, integrity and honor.
- Trustees must avoid situations in which personal interests might be served or financial benefits gained at the expense of library users, colleagues, or the situation.
- It is incumbent upon any trustee to disqualify himself/herself immediately whenever the appearance or a conflict of interest exists.
- Trustees must distinguish clearly in their actions and statements between their personal philosophies and attitudes and those of the institution, acknowledging the formal position of the board even if they personally disagree.
- A trustee must respect the confidential nature of library business while being aware of and in compliance with applicable laws governing freedom of information.
- Trustees must be prepared to support to the fullest the efforts of librarians in resisting censorship of library materials by groups or individuals.
- Trustees who accept library board responsibilities are expected to perform all of the functions of library trustees.

Adopted by the Board of Directors of the American Library Trustee Association and the Public Library Association, July 1985.

Amended by the Board of Directors of the American Library Trustee Association, July 1988, and approval of the amendment by the Board of Directors of the Public Library Association, January 1989.

Reprinted with permission from the American Library Association.

Appendix G

Selected Resources

Library Periodicals

American Libraries. Chicago: American Library Association, free monthly as an ALA member.
ILA Reporter. Chicago: Illinois Library Association, free bimonthly as an ILA member.
Library Journal. New York: Bowker, semimonthly.
Miller, Ellen G. "Advocacy ABCs for trustees," *American Libraries,* September 2001, pp. 56-59.
_____. "Getting the Most from Your Boards and Advisory Councils," *Library Administration & Management,* Vol. 15 No. 4, Fall 2001, pp. 204-13.
Public Libraries. Chicago: American Library Association, free quarterly as a PLA member.
United for Libraries Newsletter. Chicago: United for Libraries: the Association for Library Trustees, Advocates, Friends and Foundations, free to members,

Organizations
NATIONAL

American Library Association (ALA)

American Library Association, the oldest and largest library association in the world, which includes United for Libraries: the Association for Library Trustees, Advocates, Friends and Foundations (supports, encourages, and provides information for trustees of libraries) and the Public Library Association (strengthens public libraries and their contribution to the communities they serve).

American Library Association
50 E. Huron St.
Chicago, IL 60611-2795
phone: (312) 944-6780 or 800-545-2433
fax: (312) 944-3897
http://www.ala.org

American Library Association Washington Office

The ALA Washington Office is charged with tracking and influencing policy issues, legislation, and regulations of importance to the library field and the public.
ALA Washington Office
1615 New Hampshire Ave., 1st floor NW
Washington, DC 20009-2520
phone: (202) 628-8410 or 800-941-8478
fax: (202) 628-8419
http://www.ala.org/washoff/

Urban Libraries Council (ULC)

Urban Libraries Council is an association of public libraries in metropolitan areas and the corporations that serve them.
Urban Libraries Council
125 S. Wacker Dr., Ste. 1050
Chicago, IL 60606
phone: (312) 676-0999
fax: (312) 676-0950
http://www.urbanlibraries.org

STATE

Illinois Library Association

Illinois Library Association (ILA) is an independent not-for-profit professional organization dedicated to the advocacy of libraries and the furthering of the library profession through continuing education, relevant publications, marketing activities, and networking opportunities. Established in 1896, ILA encompasses membership ranging from students to trustees to library assistants as well as librarians. It is the third largest state library association in the nation, with members in academic, public, school, government, corporate, and special libraries.

Illinois Library Association
33 West Grand Ave., Suite 401
Chicago, IL 60654-6799
phone: (312) 644-1896
fax: (312) 644-1899
http://www.ila.org

Illinois State Library

Established in 1839, the Illinois State Library fulfills a twofold mission: to serve as the library for state government officials and employees and to coordinate library services throughout the state.

As the library for state government, the Illinois State Library maintains a collection of more than five million items, with strengths in the areas of government, public policy, transportation, education and other topics of interest to state government. The state library collection includes:

- an extensive maps collection, one of the largest in the country.
- Illinois State government publications. In its Illinois Documents Program, the library catalogs and retains three copies of every Illinois state government publication; one of these copies is archival, non-circulating. Additionally, the library distributes thirty+ copies to other Illinois depository libraries in the state and selected libraries beyond the state's boundaries.
- access to all federal documents, tangible and electronic, that are distributed by the U.S. Government Printing Office. The state library is one of fifty-three regional depository libraries in the country.
- information on patents and trademarks. The Illinois State Library is one of eighty-six Patent and Trademark libraries in the country.
- works by Illinois authors.
- the Talking Book and Braille Service, a division of the Illinois State Library, is a network that consists of the regional in Springfield and five talking book centers that provide a full range of library services specializing in braille and talking books.

State library staff members respond to all types of reference inquiries relating to activities of state government and provide research facilities for on-site use by state employees. All resources of the Illinois State Library are accessible to the citizens of Illinois either through their local library or by visiting the state library in Springfield. The state library participates in the ILLINET Online shared online catalog and OCLC to make its collection available in Illinois and beyond.

Through the Illinois State Library, the Secretary of State/State Librarian awards grants to local and regional library institutions to enhance, improve, and supplement local initiatives. These programs include:

- formula based grants to public libraries, school libraries and library systems;
- competitive grant programs for public library construction and local literacy projects;
- funding for library technology initiatives including computers and related equipment for use

in all types of libraries, access to electronic information resources, and support for advanced telecommunications networks and digitization of special library collections; and
- grants of federal funds to local libraries under the Library Services and Technology Act.

Illinois State Library (ISL)
300 S. Second St.
Springfield, IL 62701-1796
phone: (217) 782-2994
phone: 800-665-5576
fax: (217) 785-4326
http://www.webjunction.org/partners/Illinois/il-topics/readyref.html

REGIONAL

Illinois library systems

In August 1965, the Illinois General Assembly established library systems "to encourage the improvement of free public libraries and to encourage cooperation among all types of libraries promoting the sharing of library resources." Today, three Illinois library systems cover all of Illinois and have built neighborhoods of library cooperation for resource sharing and mutual assistance to carry out this policy. Locally elected boards that represent the diversity of their membership govern library systems and tailor programs to reflect local needs and improve library service. Library systems help save taxpayers money and improve library service to the citizens of the state through numerous cooperative programs.

Chicago Public Library System (CPLS)
400 S. State St.
Chicago, IL 60605-1203
phone: (312) 747-4090
fax: (312) 747-4968
http://www.chipublib.org

Illinois Heartland Library System (IHLS)
425 Goshen Rd.
Edwardsville, IL 62025-3045
phone: (618) 656-3216 or 800-642-9545
fax: (618) 656-9401
http://www.illinoisheartland.org

Reaching Across Illinois Library System (RAILS)
125 Tower Dr.
Burr Ridge, IL 60527-5783
phone: (630) 734-5000
fax: (630) 734-5050
http://www.railslibraries.info

Websites

American Library Association
http://www.ala.org

Benton Foundation
http://www.benton.org

Board Source
http://www.boardsource.org

Electronic Frontier Foundation
http://www.eff.org

Illinois Library Association
http://www.ila.org

Illinois School Library Media Association
http://www.islma.org

Illinois State Library
http://www.webjunction.org/partners/Illinois/il-topics/readyref.html

Illinois State Library/Administrative Ready Reference Menu
http://www.il.webjunction.org/readyref

Institute for Museum and Library Services
http://www.imls.gov/

Public Library Association
http://www.pla.org

United for Libraries: the Association for Library Trustees, Advocates, Friends and Foundations
http://www.ala.org/altaff

Urban Libraries Council
http://www.urbanlibraries.org

NOTE

Many issues involving libraries pass through the U.S. Congress and the Illinois General Assembly each year. For current information including an overview of the legislative session and specific legislation, please go the ILA website, **http://www.ila.org/advocacy/index.htm.**

Glossary & Acronyms

A

AALL: American Association of Law Libraries. Promotes and enhances the value of law libraries to the legal and public communities, fosters the profession of law librarianship, and provides leadership in the field of legal information. http://www.aall.org.

AAP: Association of American Publishers. With some 310 members located throughout the United States, is the principal trade association of the book publishing industry. http://www.publishers.org.

Abstract: A summary of the main point of an article, as opposed to its full text.

Academic Library: Any library within a publicly or privately owned institution of higher learning.

Accredited Library School: An administrative unit (school, college, or department) in an institution of higher education offering one or more programs that lead to an ALA-accredited Library and Information Studies master's degree. The American Library Association accredits programs, but does not accredit schools.

ACRL: Association of College and Research Libraries. The largest division of the American Library Association (ALA). It is an association of academic librarians and other interested individuals dedicated to enhancing the ability of academic library and information professionals to serve the information needs of the higher education community and to improve learning, teaching, and research. http://www.ala.org/acrl.

ADA: Americans with Disabilities Act. This act gives civil rights protections to individuals with disabilities. It impacts libraries as service providers and as employers. http://www.ada.gov.

AJL: Association of Jewish Libraries. Promotes Jewish literacy through enhancement of libraries and library resources and through leadership for the profession and practitioners of Judaica librarianship. http://www.jewishlibraries.org.

ALA: American Library Association. The oldest and largest library association in the world. http://www.ala.org.

ALISE: Association for Library and Information Science Education. Promotes excellence in research, teaching, and service for library and information science education. http://www.alise.org.

ANSI: American National Standards Institute. The national clearinghouse for voluntary standards development in the U.S. http://www.ansi.org.

Appropriations: Public funds set aside for a specific purpose; an appropriation amount gives the library board the authority to spend the funds. The appropriation amount includes money that will be spent from all sources—tax levy, state or federal funds, interest, donations and endowments, and other library revenue including but not limited to fines and fees.

Appropriation Ordinance: The document that gives the corporate authority (municipality, township, library district) the authority to spend the money that will be legally received.

ARL: Association of Research Libraries. A not-for-profit membership organization comprised of the leading research libraries in North America. Its mission is to shape and influence forces affecting the future of research libraries in the process of scholarly communication. http://www.arl.org.

ARRT: Adult Reading Roundtable. Developing Readers Advisory skills and promoting reading for pleasure through public libraries in the Chicago metropolitan area. http://www.arrtreads.org/

ASIS&T: American Society for Information Science and Technology. Since 1937, ASIS&T has been the society for information professionals leading the search for new and better theories, techniques, and technologies to improve access to information. http://www.asis.org.

Assessed Valuation: A percentage of the market value which the assessor places on property for tax purposes. It includes land and buildings and improvements to buildings.

Audit: A systematic examination of the financial records of an organization conducted as a rule by an external party to verify the accuracy and determine conformance to established financial criteria. A written report of such an examination.

B

Barcode: A printed horizontal strip of vertical bars used for identifying specific items or users. The codes, which represent numerical data, are read by a bar code reader and interpreted via software or hardware decoders. In libraries, barcodes are affixed to both books and library cards to assist in circulation and collection control.

Bandwidth: The size or capacity of a data line or system.

Bibliographic Control: A systematic way of organizing materials so they can be identified and found readily by author, title, subject, or some other way.

Bibliographic Record: A set of information that describes and catalogs a book or other library material retrieved from library collections.

Bibliography: A list of documents which usually have something in common, such as authorship or relevance to a given subject.

Bond: A certificate or evidence of a debt on which the issuing governmental body promises to pay the bondholders a specified amount of interest for a specified length of time, and to repay the loan on the expiration date.

Boundaries, library: The legally defined, limited geographical area from which the library board can require tax support for the purpose of providing library service.

BPH: Blind and Physically Handicapped.

Browser: A software program that translates information from the Internet for display.

Budget & Appropriation (B&A) Ordinance: Illinois taxing districts must adopt an ordinance in order to have the authority to spend the funding the library receives. The budget portion is the plan of proposed expenditures and the resources/income to be used to fund the proposed expenditures. The appropriation portion is the taxing districts' legal authorization to incur debt/obligations and to pay those obligations/debts. The B&A must be annually adopted/approved by the fourth Tuesday of September. See also Tax Levy Ordinance..

Budgeting: The development of a plan for the coordination of revenue and expenditures.

Bylaws: A law, ordinance, or regulation made by a public or private corporation, or an association or unincorporated society, for the regulation of its own local or internal affairs and its dealings with others or for the government of its members.

C

CAA: Chicago Area Archivists. Since 1982, the Chicago Area Archivists has worked to provide opportunities for local archivists, historians, librarians and others in the Chicago metro area to meet together for discussion, social interaction, and education. http://chicagoarchivists.org

CALL: Chicago Association of Law Libraries. A chapter of the American Association of Law Libraries. A nonprofit organization comprised of law librarians and other information professionals in the greater Chicago area. It was formed as a chapter of the American Association of Law Libraries (AALL) in 1947 to promote librarianship and information services, to develop and increase the usefulness of law libraries and to foster a spirit of cooperation among the members of the profession. http://www.aallnet.org/chapter/call.

Call Numbers: The classification numbers of an item of library material, used to mark the item, shelve it properly, list it in the catalog, and enable the patron to find it. The Dewey Decimal and the Library of Congress are two classification systems.

CAML: Chicago Area Museum Libraries. CAML is a networking group of museum libraries in the Chicago area. For more information contact Christine Giannoni, Reference & Circulation Librarian, The Field Museum Library at cgiannoni@fieldmuseum.org or call (312) 665-7887. cgiannoni@fieldmuseum.org

CARLI: Consortium of Academic and Research Libraries in Illinois. CARLI serves over 97% of Illinois higher education students, faculty and staff at 153 member institutions. Among the many benefits of CARLI membership are the I-Share integrated library system that serves 80 institutions; e-resources brokering, with over 2500 discounted subscriptions to electronic journals and other resources in FY2011; the Illinois Library Delivery Service (ILDS), offering 24-hour delivery among 141 CARLI libraries and all of the state's regional library systems; CARLI Digital Collections, using OCLC's CONTENTdm digital asset management software to host over 150 digital collections created by CARLI member institutions; and the Book Digitization Initiative, a partnership with the Open Content Alliance to provide a digitization opportunity for Illinois academic and research libraries. New initiatives at CARLI include demand-driven acquisitions of both print and electronic books.

CASL: Chicago Area Solo Librarians. A forum to help colleagues with problem-sharing and problem-solving issues that arise in a solo library environment. For more information, please contact Dangoule Kviklys. dank@panduit.com

Cataloging: The process of describing an item in the collection and assigning a classification (call) number.

CBC: Children's Book Council. A non-profit trade organization dedicated to encouraging literacy and the use and enjoyment of children's books, and is the official sponsor of Young People's Poetry Week and Children's Book Week each year. The Council's members include U.S. publishers and packagers of trade books for children and young adults. http://www.cbcbooks.org.

CD-ROM (Compact Disc Read Only Memory): A compact disc containing data that can be read by a computer.

CE: Continuing education. A program of courses or seminars for adults.

Certification: Signed document attesting to the accuracy and truth of a resolution or report.

Circulation: Circulation is the statistical total of items loaned to users. The circulation desk is the place in the library where you check out, renew, and return library materials. You may also place an item on hold, or report an item missing from the shelves.

CIS: Congressional Information Service. Provides indexing for U.S. Congressional hearings, reports, committee prints, and papers. http://thomas.loc.gov/.

Citation: A reference or footnote to a book, a magazine or journal article, or another source. It contains all the information necessary to identify and locate the work, including author, title, publisher, date, volume, issue number, and pages.

CLIR: Council on Library and Information Resources. An independent, nonprofit organization, works to expand access to information, however recorded and preserved, as a public good. http://www.clir.org.

CMS: Central Management Services. Illinois state agency responsible for telecommunications, etc. http://www.state.il.us/cms/.

CODSULI: Council of Directors of State University Libraries in Illinois.

Collection Development: A planned process of selecting, acquiring, and withdrawing library materials to provide a collection that is effective in meeting the needs of a library's community; cooperative collection development refers to a group of libraries working together in selecting and acquiring library material.

Conflict of Interest: As defined in 50 ILCS 105/3 et seq., it is having an interest in any contract or the performance of any work in the making or letting of which such public official (library director or trustee) may be called upon to act or vote. The statute also prohibits accepting or offering to receive any money or thing of value as a gift or bribe or means of influencing a vote or action.

Consortium: A group of libraries who use their collective buying power to achieve efficiency and economies of scale or who join together to provide a service.

Controlled Vocabulary: Standardized terms used in searching a specific database. These terms differ for each database.

Cooperative Collection Development: A system for coordinating selection and purchase of materials between two or more libraries to avoid unnecessary duplication and to complement the collections in particular libraries.

Copyright: A right of intellectual property, whereby authors obtain, for a limited time, certain exclusive rights to their works; in the United States, copyright is exclusively federal law, and derives from the "copyright clause" of the U.S. Constitution (article 1, section 8, clause 8), which provides the U.S. Congress with the power "to promote. . . . science and useful arts by securing for limited times to authors . . . the exclusive right to their . . . .writings. . . . "

Corporate Authority: The governing body with responsibilities to levy taxes, etc. Examples of corporate authorities are the municipal, county, township, and library district boards.

COSLA: Chief Officers of State Library Agencies. An independent organization of the chief officers of state and territorial agencies designated as the state library administrative agency and responsible for statewide library development. http://www.cosla.org.

CPL: Chicago Public Library. http://www.chipublib.org.

D

Database: A collection of information stored in an electronic format that can be searched by a computer.

Depository Library: A library designated to receive all or part of the publications of federal, state, or local governments.

Descriptor: A word that describes the subject of an article or book; used in many computer databases to facilitate searching.

Dewey Decimal Classification: A system for classifying and shelving books using a scheme of ten divisions, from 000 to 900. Each of the ten divisions contains ten subdivisions. Named after Melville Dewey, pioneer in library science.

Dial-up Access: Internet access using a modem and a telephone line instead of a high-speed data line.

Download: To transfer information from a computer to a computer disk; to transfer information from one computer to another computer using a modem.

E

E-book (electronic book): A book published and available in electronic form.

E-rate: A federal program that reimburses libraries for certain telecommunication costs.

EEOC: Equal Employment Opportunity Commission. Provides oversight and coordination of all federal equal employment opportunity regulations, practices, and policies. http://www.eeoc.gov/.

Equalization: The result of the assessed valuation being multiplied by the multiplier.

Equalization Factor (the multiplier): The number that is used to make property assessments uniform throughout the state. Corporate authorities are assigned multipliers by the Illinois Department of Revenue.

E & A: Educate and Automate grants are available to all types of libraries, provided they are members of a regional library system. The primary focus of the state funded Educate and Automate grant is to purchase equipment based on grant categories.

Equalized Assessed Valuation (EAV): The finalized property value once the multiplier is factored with te assessed valuation. The county clerk uses the EAV to determine the property taxes for a taxing district.

ERIC: Education Resources Information Center. A national information system established to provide access to research and development reports relevant to education. http://eric.ed.gov/.

Ex Officio: 'Because of an office.' As applied to mayors and other officials serving on boards of trustees of libraries; provides full membership without a vote.

Expenditure: The expenses involved in running the library including salaries and wages, library materials, utilities, etc.

F

Fiber-optics: A data line that uses pure strands to carry light, as opposed to copper wire, which carries electrical impulses. Though more expensive than copper wire, clean data transmission and reduced maintenance costs are the result.

FICA: Federal Insurance Contributions Act. Under the provisions of FICA, an equal amount is paid by the employer and the employee (now 7.65 percent each, of which 1.45 percent goes to Medicare). http://www.ssa.gov.

Find-It! Illinois: Web portal to Illinois governmental and library information. http://finditillinois.org.

Firewall: A gateway used to protect a server or a network from unauthorized access. A firewall generally consists of both hardware and software components.

FTE: Full-time equivalency. A measure used in human resources to indicate the number of full-time workers who would be employed if the hours worked by all employees (full and part-time) were added together and divided by the number of hours in the library's standard work week; if the library's work week is 40 hours per week, two people each working 20 hours per week equals one FTE.

FTRF: The Freedom to Read Foundation. Established to promote and defend the right to express ideas without governmental interference, and to read and listen to the ideas of others; to foster libraries and institutions wherein every individual's First Amendment freedoms are fulfilled; and to support the right of libraries to include in their collections and make available any work which they may legally acquire.

G

GILS: Global Information Locator Service or Government Information Locator Service. GILS is an open, low-cost, and scalable standard for searching basic information descriptions. It's designed so that organizations can help searchers find collections of information, as well as specific information in the collections.

Gopher: A menu-driven computer system that allows you to access information on the Internet.

H

Hardware: The bolts, nuts, boards, chips, wires, transformers, circuits, etc., in a computer; the physical components of a computer system.

HECA: Higher Education Cooperation Act. Grants funds administered by the Illinois Board of Higher Education.

Hold: A "hold" or reserve guarantees that a book checked out to another person will be saved for you when it is returned. "Holds" on any regularly circulating library materials may be placed through the circulation or check-out desk and, in many libraries, online.

Holdings: The materials of all types owned by a library.

Homepage: The first page a user sees at an Internet website.

HSLI: Health Science Librarians of Illinois. A statewide organization for librarians and others interested in health sciences. HSLI promotes professional and educational development of its members. HSLI strives to strengthen multitype library cooperation within the state and the region. http://hsli.org.

HTML: Hypertext Markup Language. The "language" or technique used to create Internet web pages.

Hyperlink: A predefined linkage between associated concepts or chunks of information, such as words or graphics in a document, that leads the reader to the related text when the hyperlink is selected. (See also Hypertext.)

Hypermedia: Various forms of information, such as text, graphics, video, and voice, used as elements in a hypertext system.

Hypertext: The dynamic linking of associated concepts among and within documents, so that the reader can easily move from one concept to another related concept. An example could be any computerized document that can lead the reader to various related information through hyperlinks.

I

IAECT: Illinois Association for Educational Communication and Technology. IAECT is dedicated to the improvement of teaching and learning through the effective use of media, technology, and telecommunications. http://www.wiu.edu/users/iaect/INDEX.htm.

IBBY: International Board on Books for Young People. A nonprofit organization which represents an international network of people from all over the world who are committed to bringing books and children together. http://www.ibby.org.

IBHE: Illinois Board of Higher Education. Coordinates higher education in Illinois. http://www.ibhe.state.il.us.

ICB: Illinois Center for the Book, an affiliate of the Center for the Book in the Library of Congress, is a nonprofit organization promoting books, book arts, libraries and reading in Illinois. http://www.illinoiscenterforthebook.org.

ICCB: Illinois Community College Board. The state coordinating board for community colleges; administers the Public Community College Act in a manner that maximizes the ability of the community colleges to serve their communities. http://www.iccb.state.il.us.

ICN: Illinois Century Network. The telecommunications backbone for public and private not-for-profit schools and colleges, libraries, museums, and government agencies to enhance the sharing of educational and knowledge resources by providing high-speed and cost-effective connectivity. http://www.illinois.net.

Icon: A small symbol on a computer screen that represents a computer operation or data file.

IFLA: International Federation of Library Associations and Institutions. The leading international body representing the interests of library and information services and their users; it is the global voice of the library and information profession. http://www.ifla.org.

IGI: Illinois Government Information. A search engine that indexes State of Illinois web servers. http://www.finditillinois.org.

IHLS: Illinois Heartland Library System, http://www.illinoisheartland.org.

ILA: Illinois Library Association: Provides leadership for the development, promotion, and improvement of library services in Illinois and for the library community, in order to enhance learning and ensure access for all. http://www.ila.org.

ILDS: Illinois Library Delivery System; Intersystems Library Delivery System. Dedicated surface delivery system funded by the Illinois State Library.

Ill. Comp. Stat. Ann.: *Illinois Compiled Statutes*, the general and permanent laws of the State of Illinois, recodified under Public Act 86-523 and Public Act 87-1005.

ILLINET: Illinois Library and Information Network. Formed in 1975, this cooperative alliance shares resources to fill the needs of library patrons. http://www.webjunction.org/partners/Illinois/il-topics/readyref.html.

ILLINET Interlibrary Loan Code: The rules governing interlibrary loan within the ILLINET libraries. The revised code was approved by the Illinois State Library Advisory Committee, endorsed by the Illinois library systems, and adopted by the Illinois State Library, effective September 2000.

ILS: Integrated Library System. The library automation system used to track items, orders made, bills paid, and patrons who have borrowed.

IMLS: Institute for Museum and Library Services. The federal agency which administers the Library Services and Technology Act (LSTA) grants and associated funding. http://www.imls.gov.

IMRF: Illinois Municipal Retirement Fund. IMRF was established under statutes adopted by the Illinois General Assembly and governed by a board of seven trustees who must also be participating members. Many, but not all, Illinois public libraries participate in IMRF. Employers and employees contribute to the fund. http://www.imrf.org.

Intellectual Freedom: The right of individuals to exercise their freedom of inquiry, exclusive of invasion of privacy; this right is supported by the American Library Association and individual libraries through their commitment to principles expressed in the *Library Bill of Rights* and *The Freedom to Read* statement.

Interlibrary Loan (ILL): A service that allows you to borrow materials from other libraries through your own library.

Internet: The international network of computer networks which provides three basic services: electronic mail, or e-mail, an online message service between computer users; remote logon, which is the ability to connect to and use services on computers at other sites; and file transfer protocol, or FTP, which allows users to move files from one computer to another. (See also WWW.)

Illinois Funds: Provides custodians of public funds with an investment opportunity which enables the custodians to earn a competitive rate of return on fully collateralized investments, while maintaining immediate access to invested funds. http://www.treasurer.il.gov/programs/illinois-funds/illinois-funds.aspx.

IRA: International Reading Association. A professional membership organization dedicated to promoting high levels of literacy for all by improving the quality of reading instruction, disseminating research and information about reading, and encouraging the lifetime reading habit. http://www.reading.org.

iREAD: Illinois Reading Enrichment and Development. The summer reading program sponsored by the Illinois Library Association. http://www.ila.org/iread.

ISBE: Illinois State Board of Education. Sets educational policies and guidelines for Illinois public and private schools, preschool through grade 12, as well as for adult and vocational education. http://www.isbe.state.il.us/.

ISBN: International Standard Book Number. A unique numerical identifier for each book or monograph publication.

ISL: Illinois State Library: The agency which serves the library and information needs of all branches of state government and, as a libraries' library, provides backup interlibrary loan and reference as well as consultative services for libraries of all types in the state. The state library coordinates the statewide library network and administers state and federal programs of financial assistance. http://www.cyberdriveillinois.com/departments/library/about/committees/home.html.

ISLAC: Illinois State Library Advisory Committee. Established by Illinois law, the committee includes not only representatives from all types of libraries, but also other individuals who represent groups of library users. http://www.webjunction.org/partners/Illinois/il-topics/readyref.html.

ISLMA: Illinois School Library Media Association. Promotes lifelong learning by the students of Illinois. ISLMA will provide leadership and support for the development, promotion, and improvement of school library media programs and the school library media profession in Illinois. http://www.islma.org.

ISN: Illinois Satellite Network. A consortium of educational institutions and regional library systems who are interested in serving the needs of professional engineers, computer scientists, and technicians by offering satellite programs designed to help participants update their current skills or expand their knowledge base. http://www.engr.uiuc.edu/OCEE/isn/.

ISP: Internet Service Provider. A vendor that provides access to the Internet, plus other services such as e-mail.

L

LACONI: Library Administrators Conference of Northern Illinois. Provides opportunity for public library administrators to meet together to share experiences, discuss problems, consider solutions, and benefit from programs of common interest. http://www.laconi.org.

LAN: Local Area Network: A direct connection of computers by some type of cable.

LC: Library of Congress. A library established as the research library for the U.S. Congress, it acts as the national library. http://www.loc.gov.

Levy Ordinance: The document that specifies the amount of tax money the municipality or library district is legally entitled to receive.

Liability: A broad term meaning legal obligation, responsibility, or debt.

Liability Insurance: To contract for protection against risks resulting from the use of the premises, whether public or private, and also those risks arising out of the practice of professions, including librarianship and trusteeship.

LIBRAS: A consortium of seventeen private college and university libraries located in the Chicago metropolitan area, focusing on promoting library cooperation, continuing education, networking, and the sharing of knowledge among membership. http://www.libras.org.

Library of Congress Classification: A system developed by the Library of Congress for organizing and shelving materials based on the alphabet. It is used instead of the Dewey Decimal System in many academic libraries and other libraries with large, specialized collections.

Library System: A group of libraries of more than one type (academic, public, institutional, school, special), the cooperative activities of which are specified by a plan approved by the state librarian.

Live and Learn: a category of grants from the Illinois Secretary of State and State Librarian.

LLSAP: Local Library System Automation Program.

LSCA: Library Services and Construction Act.

LSTA: Library Services and Technology Act. Federal legislation providing funds for public library development under law; or any other nonprofit organization engaged in the provision of cooperative library services.

M

MARC: MAchine Readable Cataloging. A standard bibliographic format developed at the Library of Congress for the exchange of machine readable bibliographic information.

Menu: On computers, menu refers to a list of options available to you.

Microfilm: See Microforms.

Microforms: A reduced-size photographic reproduction of printed information on reel-to-reel film (microfilm) film cards (microfiche), or opaque pages that can be read with a microform reader/printer.

Mill Rate: The tax rate expressed in mills and applied to each dollar of equalized assessed valuation. A mill is one tenth of a cent.

MLA: Medical Library Association. Dedicated to improving excellence and leadership of the health information professional to foster the art and science of health information services. http://www.mlanet.org.

MLA Midwest: Midwest Chapter of the Medical Library Association. The MLA is dedicated to improving the quality and leadership of the health information professional in order to foster the art and science of health information services. http://midwestmla.org.

MLA: Modern Language Association. Founded in 1883 by teachers and scholars, the Modern Language Association promotes the study and teaching of language and literature. http://www.mla.org.

MLA: Music Library Association. Professional organization in the United States devoted to music librarianship and to all aspects of music materials in libraries. http://www.musiclibraryassoc.org.

MLS, MALS, MSLS, etc.: Master's degree in library science.

Modem: Computer hardware that connects a computer to other computers through a telephone line and appropriate software. (See Network).

Multitype Library Network: A group of libraries of more than one type (academic, public, institutional, school, special) the cooperative activities of which are specified by a plan approved by the state librarian.

Municipality: A city, village or incorporated town.

N

NCATE: National Council for Accreditation of Teacher Education. A nonprofit, nongovernmental organization which establishes rigorous standards for teacher education and school library media specialist programs, holds accredited institutions accountable for meeting these standards, and encourages unaccredited schools to demonstrate the quality of their programs by working for and achieving professional accreditation. http://www.ncate.org.

NCTE: National Council of Teachers of English. Works to advance teaching, research, and student achievement in English language arts at all scholastic levels. http://www.ncte.org.

NEH: National Endowment for the Humanities. An independent grant-making agency of the United States government dedicated to supporting research, education, preservation, and public programs in the humanities. http://www.neh.gov.

Network: A communication system made up of computers which are connected. This arrangement allows information transfer from one computer to another in "real time." (See also LAN and WAN).

NILRC: Network of Illinois Learning Resources in Community Colleges. One of the oldest community college learning resources cooperatives in the nation. http://www.nilrc.org.

NISO: National Information Standards Organization. A nonprofit association accredited by the American National Standards Institute (ANSI); NISO identifies, develops, maintains, and publishes technical standards to manage information in our changing and ever more digital environment. NISO standards apply both traditional and new technologies to the full range of information-related needs, including retrieval, re-purposing, storage, metadata, and preservation. http://www.niso.org.

NLS: National Library Service for the Blind and Physically Handicapped. Administers the free program that loans recorded and braille books and magazines, music scores in braille and large print, and specially designed playback equipment to residents of the United States who are unable to read or use standard print materials because of visual or physical impairment. http://www.loc.gov/nls.

NLW: National Library Week. A national observance sponsored by the American Library Association (ALA) and libraries across the country each April. It is a time to celebrate the contributions of our nation's libraries and librarians and to promote library use and support. http://www.ala.org/nlw.

Nonresident fee cards: Illinois public libraries may sell cards to persons who reside outside of the library's tax supported boundary area. (See 75 ILCS 5/4-7 for municipal libraries and 75 ILCS 16/30-55.60 for district libraries.)

NREN: National Research and Education Network. The realization of an interconnected gigabit computer network devoted to high performance computing and communications. http://www.nren.nasa.gov.

O

OCLC: Online Computer Library Center, Inc. A not-for-profit computer library service research organization providing a family of information systems to more than 6,000 libraries in the U.S. and Europe. OCLC operates online computer and telecommunications systems that support most major library activities, e.g., cataloging, interlibrary loan, acquisitions, etc. http://www.oclc.org.

OIF: Office for Intellectual Freedom (ALA). Charged with implementing ALA policies concerning the concept of intellectual freedom as embodied in the *Library Bill of Rights*, the association's basic policy on free access to libraries and library materials. The office's goal is to educate librarians and the general public about the nature and importance of intellectual freedom in libraries. http://www.ala.org/oif/.

OMA: Open Meetings Act. An Illinois law outlining the conduct of governmental business in regard to public meetings. (See 5 ILCS 120/1etseq.)

OPAC: Online Public Access Catalog. A computerized database which usually can be searched by various search methods such as author, title, subject, or call number to find out what a library owns. Online catalogs will display the call number and the location of the material.

Ordinance: A law of a municipal government or taxing entity, such as city, village, or library district.

OSHA: Occupational Safety and Health Administration. A federal agency dedicated to saving lives, preventing injuries, and protect the health of America's workers. http://www.osha.gov/.

Output Measures: Methods devised for measuring a library's performance, as determined by use of the library's resources and services.

P

Per capita: For each of the number of inhabitants of a municipality or county, as shown by the latest census; or the result of any special census taken by the U.S. Census Bureau subsequent to its latest effective census.

PLA: Public Library Association, a division of ALA, enhances the development and effectiveness of public library staff and public library services. http://www.ala.org/pla.

R

RAILS: Reaching Across Illinois Library System, http://www.railslibraries.info.

Reciprocal Borrowing: An agreement whereby two or more libraries extend borrowing privileges to each other's patrons.

REFORMA: National Association to Promote Library Services to the Spanish Speaking. Established in 1971 as an affiliate of the American Library Association (ALA), REFORMA has actively sought to promote the development of library collections to include Spanish-language and Latino-oriented materials; the recruitment of more bilingual and bicultural library professionals and support staff; the development of library services and programs that meet the needs of the Latino community; the establishment of a national information and support network among individuals who share our goals; the education of the U.S. Latino population in regards to the availability and types of library services; and lobbying efforts to preserve existing library resource centers serving the interests of Latinos. http://www.reforma.org.

Remote Access: A phrase used to describe the connection of one computer to another computer located in different places.

Reserve: A library service that manages the circulation of certain required course materials selected by instructors or professors. It is also used interchangeably with the term "Hold" in some libraries.

Resolution: A formal statement of a decision for action by the library board.

Revenue: The library's income from all sources including tax levies, fines, fees, and gifts.

RFP: A Request For Proposals to accomplish a project.

RIF: Reading is Fundamental. The nation's largest nonprofit children's literacy organization. http://www.rif.org.

Router: A kind of switch to direct traffic within a computer network or to the Internet.

S

SAA: Society of American Archivists. North America's oldest and largest national archival professional association. http://www2.archivists.org.

Serial: A library term for periodicals or magazines.

Serial Line Internet Protocol (SLIP): Software that emulates an ethernet connection to the Internet through a modem.

SILC: Statewide Illinois Library Catalog. The Statewide Illinois Library Catalog provides access to the collections of Illinois libraries through a single, easy-to-search database, with the ability to expand your search to a subgroup of Illinois libraries, all Illinois libraries, or the world through the WorldCat database.

SILRC: Southern Illinois Resources Cooperative. A not-for-profit corporation composed of members representing institutions of higher learning and library systems in the Southern Illinois area. http://www.pbworks.com.

SLA: Special Libraries Association. The international association representing the interests of thousands of information professionals in over seventy countries. http://www.sla.org.

Special Library: A library or information center of a business, an association, a government, hospital, or other nonprofit or profit institution, which provides the organization with information, library materials, and research services.

SSLI: Society of School Librarians International. Dedicated to the development of school library programs to meet the needs of a literate citizenry in an information society. http://freewebs.com.societyofschoollibrarians.

Stacks: The area where library collections are shelved.

Standards: Generally accepted criteria developed at regional, state, and national levels suggesting or requiring certain minimums deemed essential for proper operation of libraries.

Subject Heading: A term or phrase used in indexes and library catalogs to group together materials on the same topic. Also called controlled vocabulary, descriptors, or thesaurus.

T

T-1: A data line that carries information at 1.5 megabytes a second or more. T-1 lines can use either frame relay or ATM.

T-3: A data line that carries information at 45 megabytes a second or more. T-3 lines can use either frame relay or ATM.

Tax Levy: The actual amount of property tax dollars that the library board determines is needed to run the library.

Tax Levy Ordinance: The tax levy ordinance is the authorization needed by the county clerk and county treasurer's offices to calculate the overall tax rates for the taxing district. The tax levy ordinance must be annually adopted by the first Tuesday in December and filed by the last Tuesday in December. See also Budget & Appropriation Ordinance.

Tax Rate: The percentage levied for the library per $100 of equalized assessed valuation to equal the amount of the tax levy.

TDD: Telecommunications Device for the Deaf.

Technical Processing: The preparation of a book or other item for placement in a library collection so as to be readily identified and available for use.

Terminal: One station that is part of a computer system.

Thesaurus: A list of categorized terms, such as synonyms and related words.

Tort: A violation of a duty imposed by general law; a civil wrong that does not involve a contract; a legal duty owed by one person to another; a breach of that duty and harm done as a direct result of the action. Examples: negligence, battery, and libel.

Trustee: A person appointed or elected to a public library board for a specific term of office. The board functions in accordance with Illinois library laws.

TTY: Teletypewriter. A low-speed teleprinter that allows hearing impaired individuals to communicate by means of a typewriter and phone line.

U

United for Libraries: the Association for Library Trustees, Advocates, Friends and Foundations. A division of ALA which supports, encourages, and provides information for trustees of libraries. http://www.ala.org/altaff.

ULC: Urban Libraries Council. An association of public libraries in metropolitan areas and the corporations that serve them. http://www.urbanlibraries.org.

Upload: To transfer information from a computer system or a microcomputer to another computer system or a larger computer system.

V

Vertical file: Literally the upright office files used to hold pamphlets, brochures, articles, pictures, and other items most easily organized by filing.

V-TEL: Video conferencing system which uses the telephone lines to transmit picture and sound.

W

WAN: Wide Area Network: Local area networks connected together by using telephones or other types of communications equipment. (See also LAN.)

Weeding: Disposing of books and other library materials no longer up-to-date or useful to the patrons of the library. Weeding keeps a collection current, makes way for new material, and provides ongoing evaluation of the library's material and its use.

WHCLIS: White House Conference on Libraries and Information Science. A conference affiliated with the U.S. National Commission on Libraries and Information Science.

WiFi: Wireless Fidelity. A wireless technology where WiFi enabled computers can send and receive data indoors or out when within range of a base system.